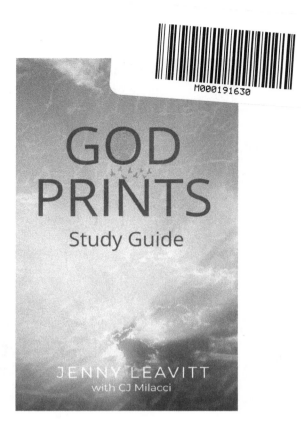

To enhance your reading experience, get your FREE GodPrints Study Guide and also receive:

- Exclusive monthly newsletters from the author
- Access to the photo vault
- Free downloadable resources
- Practical tips for discovering your own GodPrints
- And more!

PRAISE FOR

GodPrints

If you'd like to persevere in your faith in the midst of life's battles, find purpose in pain, or forgiveness for inflicted wounds, this book will be an essential step in experiencing healing and peace. Jenny's story is one of deep, abiding faith in grief and struggles, yet she includes bits of humor to lighten heavy topics. I appreciate the authenticity of Jenny's writing and vulnerability of her shared journal entries. I will not forget the many ways this book has blessed me.

Penny Cooke
Author, *Pursuing Prayer: Being Effective in a Busy World*

In *GodPrints*, Jenny Leavitt tells how life went from tragedy to tragedy. Yet through the pages, you'll see how God was always there, pointing the way to a Colossians 3:12 type of peace.

Robin Luftig
Speaker and Author, *God's Best During Your Worst*

Each one of us will experience hardships throughout our time on earth. Jenny's words resonate so deeply with my story and the stories of so many. Eventually, we are hopefully able to see God's hand working somehow in our broken stories. Let this book be your guide.

Katherine Wolf
Cofounder, Hope Heals

Jenny Leavitt's beautifully written and deeply touching book offers great blessing and comfort to help us see *GodPrints* even in the trials and sufferings of our lives. Highly recommended!

Rev. Dr. Siang-Yang Tan
Professor of Psychology, Fuller Theological Seminary
Author, *Counseling and Psychotherapy: A Christian Perspective*

Whatever difficulty you may be going through in your life, reading this book will help you get through it. Jenny describes horrible suffering and heartache and how God helped her survive. This book will encourage you to keep your faith.

Jill Roman Lord
Author of 25 children's books

GOD
PRINTS

Jenny Leavitt

Finding
Evidence of God
in the
Shattered
Pieces of Life

GOD
PRINTS
A True Story

JENNY LEAVITT

REDEMPTION
PRESS

CONTENTS

PROLOGUE

Even in sleep, I could feel my brows pull together as I watched the scene before me unfold. Suspended in some weird space, I watched as a spotlight illuminated a darkened room. I recognized the figure curled up in bed, sobbing. Weeping. It was me crying out, "God, where are you? Why can't I feel you? Why can't I feel that you're nearby? That you're with me? Like you were right after the accident? I want to feel you like that again, Lord."

Tears welled up in my eyes as I remembered the utter despair that I felt that day. The loneliness. Crying out to God for relief, for comfort. Then my eyes were drawn to what I had not known or seen that day. In that very same room, a battle was taking place—right around me.

I hadn't even known.

Hadn't even sensed it.

Yet I could see it clearly now. Fierce, angelic warriors were bravely defending me from an onslaught of evil demonic beings. As they shielded me, trying to remain as close to me as possible, demon forces waged warfare against them to get to me. When they realized they couldn't physically harm me, they changed tactics, and I watched as their lies hissed through the air and whirled around my protectors to infiltrate my mind.

Hell was snarling lie after vicious lie to me, yet I didn't see it for what it was. I really thought they were my own thoughts. What deception! And I fell for it. Over and over, the verbal assault came, whispering, "That's right. you're all alone. He doesn't care. He doesn't love you. you're not worthy. All those times that you failed him, that you sinned. You knew better. Who are you? You're nothing—you're not really his daughter."

Each word, each accusation was like a knife cutting into my heart.

As I pondered the dream, I remembered a different day and a different accident in 2013 when I'd been rear-ended and my son Jacob was battling guilt over his part in me being on the road later than usual. I told Jacob that day, "Don't do that to yourself. Do you think God was sleeping? Do you think he was unaware of what was going on? No. He knew and he was with me."

So many things could have gone wrong that day. I could have slammed into the vehicle across the median, causing further damage and injury. If the off-duty EMT didn't insist that I stay laying down in the broken seat until they could stabilize me, I could've injured myself further.

But those things didn't happen. He was with me. He was always with me.

Through those challenging early years of marriage.

Through our family's financial devastation.

Through my husband's grueling back surgeries.

Through my ravaging battle with cancer.

Even through the desperate grief of losing my son.

I see evidence of him marking my story from beginning to now—GodPrints.

God was always with me. He's with me still.

Not to us, O LORD, not to us,
but to your name give glory,
for the sake of your
steadfast love and
your faithfulness!
Psalm 115:1

GODPRINTS

YEARS BEFORE THE 2015 ACCIDENT that took Jacob's life and almost took Caleb's, my husband, Myron, preached a message on recognizing the footprints of Satan in our lives. After the accident and our loss, I would often think of the flip side of that—recognizing the handprints of God in our lives.

I heard it said once, "If you look for God's hand, you will find it." But it's not always that simple. Some days, we must make a choice to think about life and truth. We must choose what our minds dwell on. Otherwise, you'll always find what you're looking for.

Buzzards are birds that look for death and dead things. Hummingbirds are birds too. But the similarities end there. Hummingbirds look for sweet nectar. You know what? Both always find what they're looking for.

After enduring hardships and loss that I never imagined I'd make it through, I made a choice to start looking for 'GodPrints' in our story. I thought immediately of the little girl in our church who'd lost the fight to brain cancer just two months before we lost Jacob. When she passed, Jacob and I had an entire conversation about what we would want at our Celebration of Life service. I had no idea that I'd need that knowledge so soon.

We did our best to make sure Jacob's service was upbeat—a time of remembering the gift Jacob was to all of us. We tried to honor his wish that while we sorrowed for his absence, we rejoiced that he made it all the way home to heaven. That's what he told me he wanted—just two months before he died.

There was also the way God prepared Jacob to meet him personally by renewing his commitment to him at the summer youth camp just weeks before the accident. His notes, Bible, and journal from that time show a conscious effort to turn toward God and bring him back to the rightful first place in Jacob's life—followed closely by a renewal to care about others.

His memorial service was filled with stories of lives he touched just by being Jacob. He showed how much he believed this by the life he lived. Story after story emerged of his care and concern for others. He showed that he believed that we are each made in the image of God and therefore of unimaginable worth.

Another GodPrint was in January of 2015, when a visiting evangelist told Jacob, "Son, God wants you to know that he's heard your prayer. Your life will leave a long-lasting legacy for his name's sake and his kingdom."

While this alone is astounding, it was even more so when our pastor and close friend, Ron Meyer, pointed out before the graveside service, "How can someone leave a legacy unless they die?"

Even in that comforting word to Jacob, we could glimpse God's hand of preparation and care.

There's also how God prepared me that same summer. I worked through an intensive personal Bible devotional that reminded me how good our Father is and how he can heal the deep, forgotten, or neglected areas of our life. I had no idea how much I needed that thorough cleansing and renewal to be prepared for the trauma to come.

One of my journal entries from that time was dated July 14, 2015—just six weeks before we lost Jacob:

> *Thank you for blessing me in so many ways. Thank you for this abundant life you've given to me. Just like I told Jacob the other day, when I think of all I've experienced in this life, it is amazing what you've done in me and through me in these 39 years. Thank you so much, Lord. Though at times I feel so unworthy, Your grace and love have never left me.*

If God had shown me what path my life would take when I started on the walk of faith with him as a teenager, I would've said, "Um, no thanks."

No wonder he gave me that verse about never leaving me nor forsaking me. He wanted me to walk with him daily, learning to follow him.

Sometimes I can feel like I'm stumbling through life, but then when I look back, I can see that there was some logic to it. It's in those times that I'm glad he's in control. He knows and was preparing us all along—gently guiding us toward the right paths, redeeming our wasted past in the process.

And somehow, he takes those bad decisions and times I wrested control from his hands and still works something good out of it. Even if it's just teaching me something.

I know I'm not going to unravel years of stupid decisions and bad habits overnight. It's going to take time, persistence, and lots of inviting God into every part of my life daily. But if I do this? The rewards are endless.

The same is true for you, dear reader. I'm sure that if you were to look back on your life, you would see GodPrints of your own. A sermon you heard preached. A song that played at just the right moment. A conversation with a friend. A family vacation. A prayer, a word, a book.

Sometimes I think of life as a giant tapestry. God sees each of our lives from his vantage point outside of time, like seeing the finished tapestry from the top. We see the ugly underside that we're currently in. We have no idea how each of these threads is weaving together. We can't comprehend how anything beautiful could ever come from such brokenness.

But our God specializes in transformation and creating beauty from ashes. The longer I walk with him, the more I am convinced that nothing we go through is wasted in God's kingdom. Nothing.

He can redeem anything. Good grief—he took death and turned it into life.

He can certainly take my life, offered up to him, and make something beautiful out of it.

He can certainly take our marriage, our family, our church, and make something beautiful out of each.

The same is true for the threads of your tapestry—a beautiful masterpiece, woven together by him.

These past reference points, these GodPrints, have become a source of hope for the future. He was there then, he's here's now, and he'll be there tomorrow too.

Psalm 139:10 (NKJV) tells us: "Even there Your hand shall lead me, and Your right hand shall hold me."

Wherever "even there" is for you right now, be careful to look for his GodPrint in your story, knowing that you are held close in the Father's right hand.

What's Wrong with Me?

SOME DAYS ARE JUST PIVOTAL points in our life. Days when we clearly remember everything. Where we were. What we were doing. Who we were with. Even the sights and sounds come rushing back as if we were in the moment now. If you were alive on September 11, 2001, you know what I mean.

Caleb's third birthday was one of those days in my life. While Myron was at work that cool spring day, I'd already bathed and dressed the boys for a night of birthday celebration with the family at Chuck E. Cheese. I was blessed to be able to stay at home with our sons Jacob and Caleb for those formative first years of life. Doing my makeup in the bathroom mirror, I remember thinking, *Huh, I think my eyes look yellow.*

Turning side to side, I couldn't tell for sure, so I stepped out to ask Myron. He said, "No, I don't think so. It's probably just the lighting in here."

Late afternoon was quickly fading into evening, so I thought, *Okay, that's possible.*

I'd experienced all sorts of weird symptoms since giving birth to Jacob the previous November. I was misdiagnosed several times as they tried to figure out what was going on. Initially, the medical community's go-to answer was post-partum issues. But as the intensity and frequency of the unusual and seemingly unrelated symptoms increased, they began to be more diligent in discovering the cause.

Looking back now, I can see how they probably never suspected cancer. I was only twenty-two, and even though I was overweight, I was healthy. I had no known family history of cancer other than prostate on my dad's side, which obviously does not affect me as a female.

Initially, I chalked up a lot of the symptoms to being physically out of shape. Shortness of breath going to the mailbox? Yes, I really need to get this baby weight off. Itchy, dry skin? Guess I need to hydrate more and use moisturizer.

But then my pupils started acting funny. One would be dilated while the other remained normal or even anisocoria—extremely small. Have you ever taken your car to the mechanic for an issue only to have it purr like a kitten when he's trying to diagnose it? That's what my pupils would do. I'd tell the doctor about them, they'd set up an appointment, but by the time it rolled around, my eyes were both normal again.

One of the worst parts were the headaches that would wake me up almost every night with severe, debilitating pain. Twice Myron awakened to a loud noise just to find me passed out in the hallway. The only thing I remember was getting out of bed in the dark to take some medicine for the killer headache. We found out later that there was a large tumor sitting on top of the jugular vein in my chest. Every time I laid down, the tumor compressed the vein, which then blocked blood flow to my brain and eyes. Thus, the headaches and pupil variations. To this day, I have severe dry eye as a result and have not been able to wear contact lenses.

When I started passing out from the headaches, they sent me for an MRI of the brain. I can still recall the excruciating pain of laying on that flat table with my head in one position for forty-five minutes. I also still recall when I shared with our pastor, who had been praying for me, "Pastor, great news. I received the results of the brain MRI and there's nothing there."

His eyes crinkled in amusement as he said, "Jen, you may want to reword that statement."

"What? Oh. Duh. I meant there's no tumor or anything."

Gotta be able to laugh at yourself, right? Because sometimes the only alternative is to bawl like a baby, wallowing in despair.

As the spring of 1998 rolled by and the doctors couldn't find anything significantly wrong with me, I started to question myself.

Am I overreacting or imagining things? Am I really that out of shape?

But by the time we returned from Caleb's third birthday celebration and I looked in the mirror again, it was obvious that something serious was going on. No doubt about it.

The normal white sclera around my blue eyes was yellow.

I had jaundice.

I'd only seen it once before and that was not a good reference point. An older gentleman in our church developed jaundice at the end stages of liver failure right before he *died*.

I was quarantined for Hepatitis C even though I'd never done drugs, been sexually promiscuous, or any of the other things that cause people to contract the infection. When those tests came back negative, I was freed from quarantine, but left with unresolved questions.

There was no choice but for the doctors to recognize that something was going on beyond hormonal imbalances and weight issues.

*God will use suffering to teach us different things. It's
hard to teach stuff under the shower of blessing.*
—Jacob's personal notes from Pastor Stacey Dillard's sermon,
"Twice the Man"
4/2/2013

FOUNDATION OF FAITH

LET'S GO BACK TO WHERE I first discovered my foundation of faith. Myron and I met when I was sixteen and he was twenty. The church we both attended was small at the time—as in fifteen-to-twenty-people small.

One beautiful Saturday morning in April of 1992, Myron and our pastor's son, Jeremy, knocked on our family's door to invite us out to a little concert they were putting on in our neighborhood park that night.

I found out later that just three years prior, Jeremy had been riding his bicycle and was hit by a drunk driver and was declared dead on the scene. His father—our very own pastor and dear friend, Ron Meyer—rushed over to him, laid his hands on his son, and prayed for a miracle. God granted it, and to this day, Jeremy is a walking, medical miracle of God's healing power to raise the dead.

As I sat there at the concert that night watching Myron and Jeremy's little group perform Christian rap music to an accompaniment track, something inside me stirred to life. I had spent the last year going to all kinds of different churches with friends, trying to find *something*. I just wasn't sure what that something was. As I watched their Rocky Balboa drama skit unfold, I just *knew* that *this was it*.

I had been praying and asking God to lead me to a church with young people that loved Jesus and wanted to do something for him. Well, here were young people close to my age doing something with what they believed and trying to make a difference for Jesus.

I stayed after the concert to talk to them, went to church the next day, and have been a part of this wonderful fellowship of churches ever since. Our faith brought us together. And our faith has kept us together during our darkest days.

This was one of those darkest days that I was reminded of our foundation of faith.

"Let's pray," Myron said, gathering my hands into his.

I nodded, unable to speak. I was terrified. I was moments from the first upper endoscopy they did to place a stint in my pancreas in hopes of relieving the jaundice symptoms while they determined what was going on with my body. I had already had more medical procedures in the past few months than in my entire life.

It was supposed to be an outpatient procedure, so we found a babysitter for the boys and Myron took me to the hospital. That was my first experience with an overwhelming sense of fear. The thought of the doctor putting tubes, cameras, and medical devices down my throat just about sent me over the edge with anxiety.

Back then, it was common practice to use a sedative instead

of anesthesia for those types of procedures. They prepped my IV, Myron and I prayed together, and they came to wheel me into the OR. The next thing I knew, I woke up in a hospital room, not in a recovery room.

I was still very disoriented, but saw Myron sitting in the chair next to the bed. In a scratchy voice, I asked him, "Why does my throat hurt so bad?"

"Because you fought the doctors and yanked the tubes out of your throat."

"What?"

"Yep. They said you sat up right in the middle of the procedure, yanked all the tubes out of your throat, started slapping the doctor's hands away, and wouldn't let them finish. They had to restrain you, give you more sedatives, stop the procedure, and admit you. They're going to try again tomorrow using anesthesia to put you completely under."

I was so embarrassed. I didn't remember doing any of that.

Unfortunately, now I had to deal with the fear that still lingered for another twenty-four hours. Myron and I talked and prayed again, and the anxiety lessened as I chose to ask Jesus for help. Sometimes all I could do was just say his name because no other words would come.

The next morning dawned, and they took me back to the OR, this time after I signed anesthesia consent forms. The procedure went off without a hitch and the doctor was able to place the stint. They repeated that process every time I needed to have the stint replaced after that.

I was sent for a CT scan which confirmed the doctor's suspicion of a pancreatic tumor. Initially, they didn't think it was cancerous, but told me that they needed to biopsy it to be sure. They were concerned that by opening me up and exposing the tumor to oxygen, it could cause any cancer that was present to spread. The alternative was a totally new and foreign concept for me.

I had to lie completely flat on my back on a cold, steel table in a room all by myself, almost completely naked. They scanned my body and then came into the room to mark the spot where my pancreas was. Medical workers used a long syringe-type tube to forcefully push down into my abdomen and pull out cells from my pancreas.

I remember laying there with tears streaming down my face, but I couldn't move. I couldn't make any noise or any sound. I was so scared, and the pain was so great that it threatened to overwhelm me. The only thing I could think to do to help calm my anxiety was to sing praise and worship songs from church in my head, over and over again as the procedure dragged on.

On a Friday afternoon in March, I received the call. The test results were in.

"I'm sorry to tell you this over the phone, Mrs. Leavitt, but timing is critical. I'm afraid the test revealed that it's cancer."

The word alone put fear in my heart. Images of frail bodies, devoid of hair from treatment to save a life, filled my mind. People like me enduring untold pain, only to lose the battle and succumb to death.

I sat there for a minute trying to process this life-changing news.

"Mrs. Leavitt, are you there?"

"What? Oh yes, I'm here. Can you say that again, please?"

The doctor went on to explain that they would be surgically removing as much of the tumor as possible, as soon as possible.

"Mrs. Leavitt, with your permission, I'd like to send you to Gainesville for an evaluation and to start treatment immediately. I have never treated a patient as young as you, but they see patients from around the world and of all ages and I believe that would be the best for you."

To this day, I appreciate the doctor's honesty and integrity in telling me that. He could have used me as a guinea pig of sorts to learn from, but instead, he chose to do what was best for me.

He was right about the Shands Gainesville Cancer facility. I was amazed to see kids there—some as young as six or seven—wearing scarves while undergoing chemotherapy alongside patients from around the world fighting through similar diagnoses as me.

The doctor said that I needed to be ready to go to Gainesville as soon as everything was set up. Since they still assumed the cancer was localized to my pancreas, plans were put in place to proceed with surgery.

In the meantime, the symptoms worsened—the wheezing and the headaches. I took to sleeping propped up on several pillows or sitting in the living room, as that seemed to be the only way to relieve the tension.

Finally, one of the doctors ordered a simple chest X-ray to see what might be causing the shortness of breath.

On another Friday, this time in April, the phone rang again.

"Mrs. Leavitt. I am so sorry to tell you this over the phone, but the chest X-ray shows that you have multiple tumors in your chest. We need you to come to Gainesville for a biopsy, Monday if you can."

What on earth is going on? It was surreal.

*"LORD, help!" they cried in their trouble, and he
saved them from their distress. He led them from the
darkness and deepest gloom; he snapped their chains.
Let them praise the LORD for his great love and for
the wonderful things he has done for them.*
Psalm 107:13–15 (NLT)
(Handwritten note in Jacob's Bible next to this verse says,
"Practice it!" [10/22/14])

4

METASTASIZED

A WEEK AFTER I WAS diagnosed with cancer, Myron's job let him go.

He had been hired right before Jacob was born, fewer than six months before, and was laid off because they were "downsizing." It seemed so cold and heartless at the time, but God knew that in the coming months, I would desperately need Myron's strength and presence near me.

Myron is an innovative and hard worker, so he quickly set up a small home repair business that met our needs while allowing him to be there for me. It was the perfect solution for that stage of our lives and allowed him to accompany me to all of my appointments and treatments that year.

The Monday morning following that dreadful call, we were in Gainesville for another biopsy—this time of my chest. The plan was for them to biopsy the tumor right behind my sternum. When I woke up in recovery and felt like I was having a heart attack, it freaked me out.

The pain was so unexpected and overwhelming that I cried out to the nurse, "My heart. What's going on with my heart? It hurts so bad."

She told me, "The tumor was large, and it had adhered to your sternum. They were unable to biopsy it, but closed that incision and took a biopsy from the lymph node by your heart instead."

Well, no wonder it felt like my heart was hurting.

As the anesthesia wore off, the pain continued to worsen, and I began to cry in misery. They gave me morphine in my IV for the pain, even though I had a note in my chart that narcotics make me vomit. I've been told that's a side effect and not an allergy, but either way, I started violently throwing up all over the recovery room.

I pleaded with them to bring Myron back. I wanted his reassuring presence and I desperately wanted him to pray for me. Thankfully, he was allowed to come, and as I leaned into his strength and the knowledge that he would go to bat for me, they gave me anti-nausea medicine and I finally rested. Thank God, that has never happened again.

Our church family was praying for me every service, and we were believing God for complete healing. Myron and I had been searching our hearts, our motives, anything that might have given Satan a foothold in my life. We'd come up empty but were willing to accept that maybe we needed an outside spiritual assessment, so we'd asked Pastor Meyer if we could meet.

I said, "Pastor, I give you liberty right now to tell me if you feel like God has spoken to you about anything that could be causing this. Seriously, if I've sinned, I'm willing to repent. I've searched my heart and don't think I have, but I'm open."

He told me, "No, sis. I've been praying and fasting about this too. I don't think it's a sin issue. I think it's an attack straight from hell."

"Okay, then," I said. "We're going to continue to fight this in prayer."

Shortly after that meeting, Shands Gainesville called and asked me to come in to discuss the test results. They took Myron and I into this cold, sterile room and seated me on a chair in the center of it. I remember thinking, *I wish this was a bench seat so Myron could be next to me and I could hold his hand, drawing strength from his steadiness.*

The doctors came in and broke the news: It was *not* pancreatic cancer. It was Non-Hodgkin's Lymphoma.

Myron and I both sat there quietly for a minute while the doctors looked at us as if they expected me to fall apart at any moment. It was the opposite, though.

After months of misdiagnoses and feeling like I was boxing the wind, I now had a real, tangible diagnosis to fight. Instead of a vague, elusive enemy, I now had a *name* to target in prayer.

"Okay," I said. "What do we do now?"

The doctors looked at me, incredulous, and asked, "Do you understand what we're saying? You have cancer in your lymph nodes that has metastasized to your pancreas."

"Yes, I understand. We understand. What's the next step now?"

"The next step is we admit you for your first chemotherapy treatment. As soon as possible."

"Okay, let's do it."

They brought in some paperwork and even gave me some tips like, "You'll want to get that long hair cut into a shorter style so that when it starts to fall out, it won't be so bad."

The discussion then moved to whether I would allow them to insert a port in my chest to make the process more efficient. I have small veins that dehydrate easily and there had already been issues with them finding a good vein. In fact, one time I was so dehydrated that the only vein they could find was in the top of my foot. Talk about unpleasant.

The decision to put the port in was made, the first chemo session was set up, and then it was time to head home and tell family and friends.

Our family history is a bit complicated, and I dreaded telling my family the news. I knew it would be a shock, but also a source of worry and fear. I was desperately trying to remain faith and hope filled and didn't want anything—or anyone—to dampen my fighting spirit.

Myron and I are both what could be called "first generation" born-again Christians. Neither one of us were raised in churches that taught the biblical way to heaven that Jesus told us about in John 3. But both of us have experienced a very personal Savior who forgave us and cleansed us of our sin. We were—and continue to be—thankful for that.

We both came into the kingdom of God with baggage. We grew up thousands of miles apart and in completely different settings. I was raised in the city; he was raised in the country. But we were both raised in homes with emotionally detached or dysfunctional family members. We honestly had no idea how to be godly parents or spouses.

My emotional baggage and insecurities have caused a lot of grief over the years—for me *and* Myron: Lifelong weight issues, a natural tendency to be introverted, struggles with fear and anxiety, acceptance, and rejection. Throw in residual effects of being raised in a home with alcoholism, and it was a recipe for trouble in life . . . and in marriage.

A friend of mine refers to these as "first world" problems. While most of the world is concerned about where they will get their next meal or how they will live another day out of harm's way, most Americans are more concerned with their image, their latest cellphone upgrade, or any other host of things that in the grand scheme of life really are trivial in comparison to basic survival.

Nevertheless, these were, and still are the real struggles that I face.

Just like Eve in the garden, our enemy hits me where I'm the most vulnerable. He studies me to see my weak spots and then whispers lies that target those doubts and insecurities. A friend once told me that the devil looks for the "chinks in our armor," because he knows that if he can't take us out completely, he can at least get us so sidetracked that we're not engaged in the fight anymore.

For me, it was whispered lies like:

Has God really said that he loves me? That I'm his daughter? That I'm forgiven? That he has plans for me? Good plans, with a hope and a future?

Sometimes I look at the Christian artwork decorating the walls of our house and I wonder how often I walk right past them because they've ceased to be meaningful to me. Some of my favorite ones remind me of who I am in Christ as his beloved daughter. How many times have I allowed the promises of Scripture to become Christian decor in my life instead of the precious reminders they were meant to be?

Too often. And that's *not* a habit I can blame on a complicated family history, as much as I'd like to. I am in charge of my own faith—a faith that would be tested more than I thought possible in the days and weeks to come.

> *Help me rejoice in this second chance of life you've given me. Please forgive me for turning so quickly to self-reliance. Help me to realign my heart with Yours, my will with Yours, my thoughts with Yours. . . . I don't trust these unstable, wishy-washy feelings to lead me. I trust you.*
>
> ~From Jenny's private journal

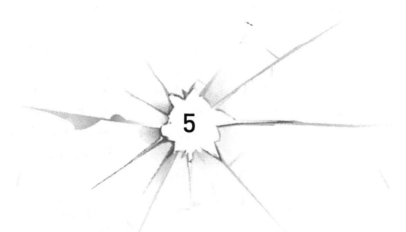

THE BATTLE FOR LIFE

THE FIRST TREATMENT SEEMED TO go well. The five days of steroids caused me to be irritable, but at least I had some energy to try to get things done. By the second treatment, though, these same steroids became a nightmare, making it almost impossible to sleep for five days while having a baby (Jacob) and toddler (Caleb) at home.

The doctor was right about my hair too. It started falling out just a little more than usual, but then quickly began coming out in clumps. One day I went in the bathroom, shut the door, and looked at my mostly bald head in the mirror. With tears streaking down my face, I shaved off the few stragglers that remained. I told Myron later that I didn't realize how much of a woman's dignity comes from her hair until mine was gone. And I mean *gone*. I had no eyebrows, no arm hair, nothing.

I tried to make light of it (because really, what else could you do except cry?), and so I said, "Hey, just think of all of the money I'm saving you on hair products now."

Myron, God bless him, assured me that he loved me anyway—hair or no hair.

Shortly after the first treatment, we were told that they needed to determine if the lymphoma had spread to my bone marrow, and since I was still in the hospital, they scheduled a bone marrow biopsy right in my room. I wouldn't even have to leave the hospital bed.

The nurse came in to explain the procedure she was about to perform. She had me roll over on my side and said, "I'm going to be placing this long needle in through your spine and extracting a bone marrow sample to send off for testing."

Myron was allowed to stay with me and was holding my hand as the nurse said, "Okay, ma'am, now you're going to feel a slight prick."

I remember thinking, There is absolutely no way this woman has ever had this done. If she had, she would never tell someone it was going to be a slight prick.

It was so painful that I arched off the bed and about ripped Myron's arm out of his socket. He stood there, sure and steady as the nurse hummed while she worked. I consider myself to be pretty patient, but I was not feeling patient with her right about then.

Thank God, the test showed no sign of cancer in my bone marrow or blood.

The chemotherapy treatments were so hard on me that I had to be hospitalized three out of the six treatments because my platelets dropped dangerously low. Twice Myron rushed me to the emergency room because the nausea, vomiting, and dehydration were so bad that I could barely lift myself out of bed.

One time in the ER, they tried to put a tube down my nose to my stomach, but I was so violently ill that I couldn't swallow the tube down like they needed me to for it to be placed properly. After admitting me, I laid there on my side, throwing up bile as the doctors stood to the side of the room with Myron, discussing me like I wasn't right there.

"Mr. Leavitt, there's no reason why this should be happening."

As if to imply that somehow, I was making myself sicker than I should be.

The violent vomiting started again just as Myron was replying, "Well, I think it's because she's never done drugs or anything, and this is hitting her system really hard."

The doctors stood there, looking shocked and said, "Wow. She really is vomiting bile."

No kidding.

On top of all of that, Gainesville was over an hour from our friends and family, so visitors were few. When they did come, they had to gown up with masks to enter my room due to my severely compromised immune system. I couldn't have fresh fruit to eat because there was too much risk of pesticides causing me problems. I couldn't receive fresh flowers for the same reason.

One time Myron bought me a dancing plastic sunflower that played the song I used to sing to our boys as babies, "You are my sunshine, my only sunshine. You make me happy when skies are gray. You'll never know, dear, how much I love you. Please don't take my sunshine away."

The boys loved that singing flower so much they eventually broke the dancing petals right off.

Another time I asked Myron to bring my keyboard to the hospital room so I could play. One of the few sweet memories I have of those dark days is sitting up in bed, the keyboard on top of the rotating bedside table, weeping as I practiced some of my favorite church songs.

Sometimes people would comment on how "strong" I was. I would simply shake my head and say, "It's only because of Jesus. He's my strength. I don't know how people go through something like this without him."

It was during those bleak days of cancer treatments that I noticed something about humanity. While I leaned on my faith for strength and peace, I looked around and I saw people facing the very real possibility of death, just like me, and lash out at God in anger for allowing it to happen. Or they would wallow in self-pity, giving in to the despondent feelings of despair and hopelessness. Still others chose to lean on their own power, limited as it was.

I realized that we humans *don't* go through something like that very successfully without Jesus.

A good friend of mine lost her brother in a drunk driving accident and told me that her pastor told her, "Life happens. You either face it with Jesus or without him." So true.

The year 1998 also made me so grateful for our loving church family and dear friends who stepped up to help us, over and over. Their help with childcare, housework, errand running, and meal prep was the only way we made it through that year.

As a brand-new believer in my teens, my favorite Scripture was, "I will never leave you nor forsake you." I clung to that verse as an anchor for my soul—a precious promise that I do not have to navigate life on my own. Then, just a few years later, cancer struck. Like an obsessed woman, I scoured Scripture looking for hope. For answers and healing. For some purpose in the pain. Significance in the struggle.

I was not disappointed.

Romans 8 became a lifeline for me. The whole chapter deals with this life of suffering compared to an eternal perspective of the future glory that waits for us if we persevere. Our fridge, bathroom mirror, and walls were plastered with scribbled scriptural reminders on scraps of paper, post-its, index cards—anything that I could find to write on.

I would be lying in bed, so weak I could barely move, and glance over at the light switch, where I'd be reminded, "All things work together for the good of those who love God and who are called according to his purpose."

Or in the bathroom, as nausea overcame me, I would see the reminder that there is "Peace that passes understanding" available to me.

Many times, these gentle reminders nudged me back to a healthy place. Mentally and spiritually.

But the toll on my body was great. The battle for life was real.

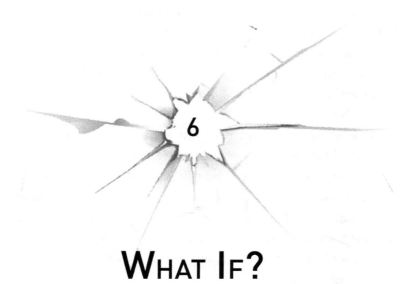

6

WHAT IF?

GOD'S FAITHFULNESS HAS ALWAYS BEEN obvious in my life. He has shown me over and over again that nothing is wasted in his kingdom. When I got saved as a teenager, I would have never imagined how that one decision would change the course of my life forever. Just like that pivotal day of March 3, 1998, there have been other pivotal moments in my life too.

The most important was March 27, 1991, when I surrendered my life to Christ and he took the weight of my sin off my shoulders, adopting me into his family.

There was another pivotal day just a year later, when I was offered a full-ride scholarship to Florida State University and was fully intending on using it. But then I told God that I was available if he was able to use my life.

That simple prayer started an entire year of wrestling with God over my future plans. Every time I would think about my life after graduation, my stomach would get tied up in knots. I just had this feeling that God was trying to steer me in another direction, but I was really scared of the fallout. I knew it would not go over well with my parents. And it was a huge leap of faith for me into the unknown. For a woman who likes structure and routine, that was a major hurdle in itself.

One night, as we watched a movie in church about three missionaries, I felt personally challenged. The film ended with, "Who will go? The need is great. Who will go?"

I went down to the altar that night, sixteen years old and weeping. I said, "God, I'm done fighting you on this. I'll do your will. If you don't want me to go to college, I won't go to college."

I've looked back on that pivotal point in my life many times and thought, *What if?*

What if . . . I'd told God that night when I felt him pressing on my heart, "No. I'm going to do what I want to do."

Then I wouldn't have married Myron and we wouldn't have had the boys.

What if . . . I had told God, "No, I don't want to listen to you. I'm going to college anyway. Plenty of people go to college. It's not a sin. What's wrong with me going?"

Then I would've been almost done with college by the time I was diagnosed with cancer.

Not only would I have walked that road alone—without Myron and the boys—but more than likely I would have never been able to have children at all. The treatments took a substantial toll on my reproductive system, and I was told, "It's a good thing you already have two children. You probably won't be able to have more."

But the most humbling, and startling *What if?*

What if . . . I had rebelled against God's will for my life and done my own will? That *one,* pivotal decision . . . Would I have survived the cancer? I really don't think so.

But by God's grace, I *did* surrender to his plan instead of mine.

And by God's grace, I *did* survive the cancer.

I want to issue a challenge to you, dear reader. What "what ifs" do you have in your own life? What decisions have you made that led you to where you are? What moments of obedience and disobedience have paved the path to your reality? And if you aren't happy with your reality, what choices can you make right now to ensure you aren't regretting your next future "what if?"

God knows that I have made more than my fair share of really stupid decisions that I would erase or redo if I could. But I am so grateful that I made the decision to surrender my future that night at church.

Because of that one choice, I did not walk through cancer alone, but with Myron and Jesus right there with me. And because of that one choice, I will never have to wonder if I could have had children after the cancer treatments took their toll. We were already the proud parents of two energetic, bright young boys who filled the house with joy and laughter.

Sure, there were lots of times that it was hard, really hard, being a parent. Trying to raise a family according to Scripture and not necessarily "the way we were raised." A lot of our styles of relating and parenting were a direct result of some of the dysfunctional methods we'd been exposed to. So of course, there were clashes, fights, disagreements . . . between the boys, but also between Myron and I as we tried to navigate our way out of our old habits and into new, Christlike ways of relating.

I have a feeling we'll be working on that until Jesus comes.

That night at the altar when I was sixteen years old is one of the most indelible GodPrints in my life. It didn't make sense at the time. But I sensed in my spirit that it was a moment I would live to remember. I was right.

ANCHOR OF TRUTH

I RUINED MY FIRST WIG. Well, really, I melted it.

I had been grilling dinner and leaned over to turn the meat when I realized, too late, that the heat singed the cute little bangs right off. I cried all afternoon as I realized that we didn't have the money to replace it.

It was a tremendous blessing when shortly after that the American Cancer Society offered a free class for cancer patients on how to wear makeup when you have no hair, and your skin is pale and chapped from treatment.

I was overcome with gratitude, as they not only gently and kindly showed us the best methods to work with what we had, but also gave us a box of high-quality cosmetics that name-brand companies had donated. They also gave me a beautiful new auburn wig that accentuated my face shape perfectly. I received so many compliments on the style and color that I tried to imitate it once my hair eventually grew back in, but was not successful and eventually gave up.

Throughout the course of the six chemo treatments, the pancreatic stints had to be replaced periodically, and every so often they would run tests to make sure the drugs were working and the tumors were shrinking.

One particularly challenging time of hospitalization, I was exceptionally weak and struggling. Unbeknownst to me, Myron was having a conversation with the doctor out in the hallway.

"Mr. Leavitt, it doesn't look like she's going to pull through this time. I suggest you get her affairs in order. Perhaps call family and friends and let them know that if they'd like to come, they need to come quickly."

In what can only be described as a "holy defiance," Myron looked the doctor straight in the eye and said, "Listen, you get back in the hospital room and you do what you do. I'm going to do what I do. Because Jenny *not* coming home is not an option."

All I knew at the time was that Myron came back in the room, pulled the chair next to the bed, and grabbed my hand. My husband is not a touchy-feely, emotional type of guy, so when I saw a tear slide down his cheek, it got my attention.

Looking intently at me, he said, "Jenny, you need to fight. I need you to fight. The boys need you to fight. I love you too much to lose you."

Stunned, I sat there just staring at him.

What on earth is going on? I've never seen him like this. Crying. For me.

He needs me and loves me. If I ever doubted it before, he's showing me his true heart now.

And he wants me to fight.

He's told folks since then, "Bad news has a way of restructuring your priorities. In the face of Jenny's cancer diagnosis, I would put on a brave face, but on the inside think, *What would I do without my wife?*"

I voiced the words that would give me a boost of strength to continue to battle this ravenous disease. "Okay, Myron, I'll fight."

Holding my hands, he prayed for me—calling out to our Father for breakthrough, for healing, wisdom, and strength.

As hard as it was to endure all of that, my most intense battle was one of the *mind*.

The constant mental assault wasn't about the cancer or even the physical toll on my body. Nor was it about the treatments or even the prospect of dying.

No, the tormenting, fearful worry wasn't for me, but for our boys.

"Oh, God," I would cry out. "Our boys are so young. How on earth will Myron be able to raise a baby and a three-year-old? I know he's a capable man, Lord. But it's too much."

One night, I had enough. Making my way in the dark to the quiet living room, I fell to my knees.

"God, I am not going to leave this place until I hear from you. I *cannot* keep going like this. Living in constant fear over our boys. Worrying about Myron. What he'll do if I die. How he'll raise two young children on his own. I just can't do it anymore, Lord. I'm not leaving until you give me peace about our boys."

I don't know how long I stayed there, crying out from the bottom of my soul for relief from the worry and fear. Releasing our boys to God. Wrestling through the anxiety that wanted to crush me, until I finally came to a place of surrender, giving everything over to the only One who could do anything about it.

God didn't take the cancer away that night. I still had to endure months of treatments that left me weak and fatigued.

He didn't physically appear to me that night either, wrapping me in his arms to dry my tears and hold me tight.

But he did show up. Another GodPrint moment.

First, it was a deep peace that settled over my soul like a warm blanket. Wrapped tightly around me, it quieted those runaway anxious thoughts. He settled my soul, letting me know he was there.

Then, in the quiet, a still, small voice was tenderly whispering to my heart, *Jenny, I love your boys even more than you do. They're mine. I will take care of them. Regardless of whether I bring you home or not.*

Sitting in stunned silence, the words soothed the frayed edges. It's hard to fathom anyone loving my boys more than I do. Yet, the God of the universe had just assured me that he did. That they're his. They always have been, always will be. As much as I'd like to think they're mine, they're not. Myron and I are just stewards over these precious lives entrusted to our care.

They were his before they were mine. They'd continue to be his, even if I died.

Sobering, but the truth. Truth that I could set an anchor in.

"All right, Lord. Thank you for hearing me. Thank you for this peace. Thank you for taking care of our boys. For loving them first. I trust you, Lord. I trust you to take care of them. No matter what happens."

When you got saved, the Word of God should shape
how you think. This will be the greatest battle you face.
—Pastor Joe Campbell (5/6/2021)

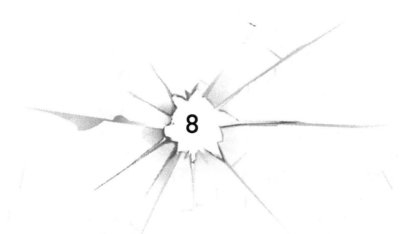

THE PHONE CALL

WITH MY TWENTY-THIRD BIRTHDAY IN August came the good news that the chemo treatments had done their job. Scans showed only scar tissue, but the doctors wanted to proceed with the radiation treatments if any residual cancer cells were free floating in my body.

One hurdle down. One to go.

Even back then, I could see God's hand—another GodPrint—in leading me to my radiation oncologist. She was already one of the best in her field, had contributed to several textbooks, and would eventually go on to be a part of the team to pioneer the UF Health Proton Therapy Institute in Jacksonville.

So not only did God lead me to a competent doctor, but he also led me to a leader in the field. To this day, she remains not only one of the best doctors I've ever had, but one of the best people I've ever known. A consummate professional with a great bedside manner, she has maintained her desire to see people cancer-free while gently presenting truth when needed.

After reviewing my file, she explained that I would need to stay in Gainesville for over a month, Monday through Friday each week, while I received intense, two-a-day radiation treatments. But first, I had to be tattooed to make the process more efficient.

I was taken to another cold, sterile room and told to undress—completely. Then I had to lay flat on a freezing table while they scanned me. A technician came in and used permanent markers to draw on all the places of my body where I would receive radiation. My husband stills jokes that he has a *biker chick* for a wife since I received sixteen tattoos that day.

The tattoos—little blue dots—were used to focus the radiation machine on the correct field quickly and efficiently.

I remember the moment it struck me during the first treatment *why* the technician had to leave the room and speak to me through an intercom—to avoid being exposed to the high levels of radiation that were being aimed at my body.

But by the end of the five weeks, I didn't even care anymore. I just wanted it all to be over.

I spent a lot of time thinking about the Scriptures on those scraps of paper or silently singing those church songs in my head. I found that to be the only way to calm the chaos in my mind and help me refocus on the only one who could be with me in that room—God.

Fifty-six times I laid there, bald, mostly naked and freezing, while loved ones and friends changed my baby's diaper and took my three-year-old to the park to play.

Fifty-six times I rode the shuttle bus back and forth from the American Cancer Society-Winn-Dixie Hope Lodge that hosted me free of charge to the radiation unit at the cancer center.

Fifty-six times I shut out the thoughts that if the cancer didn't kill me, the radiation they were shooting into my blood, bone, and marrow might.

The radiation didn't make me nauseous like the chemo, but

instead killed my appetite. On top of that, it made me so exhausted that I often slept in between the morning and afternoon sessions, foregoing meals. Since chemo is designed to kill fast-growing cells, the results were immediate. The side effects were intense at the time, as all the cells in the body that reproduce rapidly were attacked. But the radiation has proven to be almost worse for me to bear in the long run.

The radiation side effects seemed minor in 1998 when compared to the chemo. As the years have rolled by, though, I can't tell you how many times I've been told that an issue I'm dealing with or a surgery I will need to have is directly related to long-term effects of radiation exposure.

The month I spent in Gainesville, my husband would drive an hour-and-a-half every night to be with me while our friends and family would care for the boys. Then he would get up early the next morning, work all day, get the boys settled, and do it all over again. On Friday nights, he would take me home for the weekend, just to return me to Gainesville Sunday night.

I've told people that I feel like I missed Jacob's entire first year of life. Even though it was no fault of my own, I felt horrible about missing so much of Caleb's life too. I'm so grateful for the love of family, both blood-related and brothers and sisters in Christ who stood in the gap to help us.

As Jacob's first birthday drew near, we finally got the phone call that we'd been longing for.

"Mrs. Leavitt, great news. The treatments were effective, and the cancer is in remission."

With that victory report firmly in mind, I went against the doctor's recommendation in 1999 and had the port removed. For me, it was a step of faith that the cancer wasn't coming back, and I wasn't going to need the port anymore. I also donated all the wigs, scarves, and turbans to the American Cancer Society for the very same reason. At the time, I doubted if that was a wise decision. But

I felt like it was a stand that I needed to take in my own life to put the cancer behind me and move forward.

I like to say that I'm not a cancer *survivor*, I'm a cancer *overcomer*.

I wish I could say that I was always so resolute, so determined in believing that to my core.

That when the three-month check-ups came and went, I always stood firm on the promises from God's Word.

That as the months rolled by, doubts never came. That my trust in God's goodness never wavered.

That when I was told that I was going to have to start having yearly mammograms at age twenty-eight due to the increased risk of breast cancer, I held fast to my convictions that God healed me for a purpose.

I wish I could say I was always a bastion of faith, a shining example of a Spirit-filled believer.

I wish I could say that I looked back on all the GodPrints of my story and knew without a doubt that he was holding me in the palm of his mighty hand.

I wish I could say all of that. But that would be a lie.

TIME MARCHES ON

BEFORE LONG, I'D BEEN CANCER-FREE for two years. I had a renewed zeal to live life to the fullest and savor every moment of it. Spurred by the desire to make my life count, Myron and I stepped out in faith and pioneered a small church plant. We had done so before Jacob was born and felt that God was calling us to ministry again.

At that point, Caleb was five and Jacob was two. I had been healthy for almost two years when one day I lost my footing when I was stepping back out of our minivan after buckling the boys in. Arms flailing in the air, I landed entirely on my left wrist, breaking it in three places. Five days later I had to be put under anesthesia again and have four external pins with hardware placed in my arm to secure it for six weeks.

After the six weeks I went back to the doctor's office, and they unscrewed the pins right there at the table I was sitting at while I watched. They put them in a bag and told me I could take them home with me if I wanted to. I threw the disgusting things away. My arm healed and life plowed forward. Four years rolled by as the boys grew and started school.

Then one day, I received news of another impending hospital stay. The labs from my annual checkup were abnormal so a PET scan had been ordered. I'd just found out that my thyroid and one of my tonsils showed a strong possibility of cancer—most likely related to the radiation exposure. Once again, surgery was in my future.

When I shared the news with the boys that night, Jacob said, "I just don't understand, Mom. Why would they treat cancer with something that causes cancer?"

"Because there were no other options, son. When you have stage four cancer, there's not a whole lot to try. So, yeah, I've had a lot of issues from the radiation and chemo, but at least I'm still here. I'm still alive."

I've had so many surgeries over the years that I've started taking a list with me to new doctors. I told my radiation oncologist once that sometimes I feel like a "science project." I never know if my medical issues are from getting older, from chemo, or from the radiation.

I still chuckle when I think of her response to that. In all seriousness, she said, "Now, Mrs. Leavitt. Think of it as *aiding us in research.*"

I've *aided them in research* so often they asked me to sign a document agreeing to let them study my file, comparing it to other long-term survivors to find similarities.

That was a humbling visit. My doctor dropped a bombshell when she casually mentioned—as if saying "Oh, it's sunny out today"—that I developed a low-grade heart murmur. Not to worry, though. They've seen this before in cancer survivors who had treatments like mine. They'd monitor it and, if they needed to, they'd replace one of my heart valves with a pig valve.

Oh? Is that all?

Just my heart we're talking about here!

While absorbing that bit of news, the doctor casually commented, "You know, you're actually doing very well for someone who only had a 25 percent chance back in 1998."

"Umm, excuse me? Twenty-five percent chance of what?"

"Oh, did no one ever tell you? You had about a 25 percent chance of survival. So, you see, even with these issues, you really are doing remarkable this far out."

On previous visits, we'd discussed how her follow-up patients are becoming increasingly fewer over time. She no longer practices at the location where I was initially treated, but thankfully still sees her follow-up patients. She's down to just one day a month to see us though because, over time, some have simply stopped following up while others have passed away.

So, wow! This latest bit of news was shocking. Humbling.

Back in 1998, I had a 1-in-4 chance of survival. Out of the one in four, even fewer have lived as long as I have.

Why me? Why did I survive?

Have I squandered the extra years I was given?

Am I using them wisely?

While I sat in our darkened living room later, I was overcome with emotion at my second chance at life. Tears streaming down my face, I tried to put some steel in my spine to face this latest development.

Once again, I would have to "go under." Once again, I would have to battle the worry, the fear. Once again, I would have to corral my wayward thoughts and make it through the days until the call came with the biopsy results.

Is the cancer back? Is it a different kind of cancer? Is it a long-term effect of the treatment or something new? Do I need to be gearing up for battle again? Fighting for my life?

I'm not so much worried about the possibility of dying. I settled that with Christ a long time ago.

No, with each new scare, each new medical issue, there's this apprehension lurking in the background. If the cancer comes back, I'll have to go through all of that again.

The treatments, the nausea, the dehydration, the headaches. The strong, life-*saving* medications took a severe toll on my body. Designed to strike the tumors hard by targeting every fast-growing cell in my body, the drugs also killed my nails, hair follicles, platelets, and other beneficial, life-*giving* cells.

The steroids that started each treatment made me unable to sleep for days. The violent vomiting and unpredictable diarrhea that accompanied the chemo left me housebound, frail, and dehydrated, all while caring for my three-year-old and baby.

Several times when I was so overcome with pain or weakness that he was worried, Myron rushed me back to the hospital. One time, I had been vomiting so long and forcefully that the only thing left to throw up was stomach bile. My platelets were so low that I appeared pale and wan and often struggled to stay awake. My blood pressure dropped so low that a nurse once asked me, "Are you alive, honey?"

The fifty-six radiation treatments, morning and night for over a month, left me extremely fatigued to the point where I frequently slept all day.

If I wasn't in the hospital, I was sick, tired, or miserable.

It was . . . not pleasant, to say the least.

So, yeah, that was a rough year. When 1998 came to a close, and I was declared in remission, I told my husband, "Myron, I'm just telling you right now, if the cancer comes back, I'm not going through that again."

To which he replied, "Oh, yes you are. Because you love me, and you love the boys."

I struggled with that. I mean, of course, I loved him and the boys more than anything. But I was battle weary—tired of fighting, tired of wrestling through each day. After considering his words for a moment, I knew he was right.

If I had to, I would fight again. For them.

Sometimes, like today, I'm keenly aware of just who I am. All my failures, all my shortcomings. Sometimes it's so overwhelming to look inside and realize just how I am NOT you God—that it seems easier to just not look at all. If I don't look at who I am deep inside, I can avoid the issues, right? The wounds, the hurts that have never been addressed or healed. The blackness of my sins or other's sins that have affected me. The fear that I allow to grip me.

It's such a paradox, though. If I knew your heart, Father, I wouldn't avoid you. I wouldn't give in to the shame and the lie that if you could see inside me, you'd be repulsed and turn away from me.

How is it that I so quickly forget that you are GOD? You see it all, know it all . . . yet here I am again, trying to cover it up—not with leaves as they did—but maybe with being busy, even in good things. Or with any of the other things I run to instead of you.

Yet, over and over, you tell us that you love us enough to leave the ninety-nine and come after us—after me.

That you're that Father waiting at the end of the road, looking each day, for my scraggly self to come to my senses and come back to you.

Who shows me these things BECAUSE he loves me and wants to help me overcome them. By bringing them to you—the only One who can forgive me, change me, and cause the darkness to flee.

~From Jenny's private journal

Do-Overs

MYRON AND I MADE A conscious decision before we even had children to do our best to raise them on the firm foundation of the Rock of Christ. We definitely could have done a better job, but I can look back and see the GodPrints of how he helped us there too.

I've told young mothers who ask me for advice, "Don't forget the God factor. Once you get God involved in your life and your family, he takes up the slack in your parenting. Thank God. He knows and loves our kids and will help us."

I am grateful that Myron and I got saved at a young age and settled our will that we were going to serve God for the long haul.

We're flawed human beings who are going to make mistakes. That's not an excuse—it's just reality. I read a quote one time where a man had received this piece of advice from a friend when he first became a parent: "You're going to screw up your kids' lives. Just try not to screw them up too much."

While that may be funny, there is certainly some truth in it. I'm grateful that we have a Father who helps us . . . and our kids.

I'm grateful that God took two people from broken families, put us into the family of God, and helped us to build our lives on his principles. Little by little, he did his best to prepare us for what was coming.

At one point, Myron and I had been pastoring that second little church for a while and things weren't going too well. Several church startups had failed to get off the ground and closed down in the same area where we were laboring to build a church body. After one particularly trying time, Myron told me, "It makes no difference to me what happened then. God brought us here. He's doing something. He's going to establish his work here. Our job is to do everything we can and then leave the results up to God."

You know what? God honored Myron's stubborn, tenacious faith, and brought a breakthrough soon after that. It was like a neon light went off for me: "Look at this. *This* is what it looks like when a person allows God to take that stubborn, strong will and use it for his glory." Those personality traits are vital for a godly leader to bring breakthrough and deliverance, and establish dominion.

That was also when it dawned on me that all "warriors" (a.k.a. strong-willed children) have to have parents to help mold and shape those personality traits. They aren't born harnessing that God-given ability.

Caleb has known since he was little that he's named after the biblical hero Caleb, a tough, seasoned warrior who even at eighty years old was not only fighting battles, but *winning*. Caleb has also known that his name means "mighty warrior for God,"

Many times, as Caleb was growing up, we battled that stubborn strong will, sometimes constantly reminding him that he had to allow God to redeem, mold, and shape those parts of his personality into the leader God was calling him to be. In Myron, I'd seen God take a stubborn will, yielded to him, and redeem it for his glory. I knew it could happen, but Caleb would have to do his part. I can't count how many times I told him, "Filter, Caleb. Engage the filter, son." Or when he was a toddler, reminding him that *I am the adult.* You will *not* win this battle.

After a few years, Myron and I turned over the pastorate to some wonderful friends of ours who have led the congregation in growth and maturity ever since. We came back to our mother church and settled it in our hearts that we would serve God wherever and however he thought best. We just wanted to do his will. We've found that to be the only place we truly feel peace.

We'd always been fruitful and happy working with the children's ministry, and before long, it became evident that God wanted us involved in that again. We loved every minute of it. I admit that sometimes life became mundane and sometimes life got irritating. After all, we had two rambunctious little boys and very busy lives.

There were so many good times, though—treasured memories that I wouldn't trade for the world now.

I've always loved to read and began reading to our boys when they were just babies. Some of my favorite memories of that time are of us three sitting on the couch together reading *The Hardy Boys.*

Or there was the time that all four of us were enjoying an ice cream at the local Dairy Queen when in walked the doctor who had done that first endoscopy where I fought him and yanked out the tubes. I was mortified that he remembered me, but he was overjoyed to see that I not only survived the cancer, but was enjoying life with my family.

One of our family's funniest memories involved Jacob, scissors, and one of the best Mother's Day gifts I ever received. It was one of those big inflatable pools for our backyard. It was about three feet deep and several feet across. When the Florida summer hit in full swing and the boys were driving me up a wall, I'd say, "Hey, why don't you guys go in the pool?"

The boys and I loved that pool, but for very different reasons.

While Myron was out of town for a Bible conference one year, the boys were bickering, being disobedient, and trying every last bit of my patience. Much to my frustration, nothing I could do or say to discipline them was working. When Myron and I are apart, we do our best to talk on the phone daily, even if it's just to say hi.

That day, I had had enough. I called Myron and told him everything that had been going on. My husband was, shall we say, a "challenging" child to raise. He has vast experience with effective and creative discipline measures and came up with a method to occupy our boys and give them time to reconsider their ways while they were at it.

He told them each to take a pair of scissors and trim every piece of grass, by hand, that he would normally weed-eat. The boys always helped with yard work, so they knew exactly what that meant.

While still on the phone, I sent them outside, Caleb to the front yard and Jacob to the backyard.

The next thing I knew, Jacob came running back inside, out of breath and nervously asking, "Mom, do you have any tape?"

"Tape? What do you need tape for, Jacob?"

At that very moment, I heard an unidentifiable *WHOOSH* from the backyard. I turned my head to look out the sliding glass windows just in time to see the three-foot-high pool walls slowly collapse and water flood over the sides.

Jacob instantly began wailing, while Myron was asking, "What's going on?"

My brain caught up to what my eyes were seeing, and I said, "Jacob, did you cut the pool?"

"I'm sorry—it was an accident."

The pool was completely ruined.

Fast forward a few days later when Myron returned. Sitting on the couch, I listened as Myron called Jacob into the room and asked, "Son, do you want to tell me what happened?"

Our precious young son stood there, wringing his hands together, in fearful anticipation of the impending punishment. Then, with tears in his eyes, he blurted out, "Dad, I was tempted."

I had to pick up the throw pillow and hide my laughter as Myron sternly told Jacob, "Go on up to your room while your mom and I discuss your punishment."

The boys and I missed that pool, but for very different reasons. Now it's one of those memories that I treasure deep in my heart.

Dear Dad,

I want to thank you for the way that you have never given up on me, even when it seems like I'm not listening, or just don't care. That means so much and is truly an example of God's unconditional love toward us. I also want to thank you for your example-ship in how you always try to do what is right and acceptable in God's eyes, no matter the consequences that may be here on earth. I will try my hardest in the rest of this year, and for forever, to listen to your guidance and direction, and to change the things in my life that do not match up with God's word. I will try my best at these things, and with God's help, I know that I can do everything that I need to and be the godly man that I need to become. Once again, I want to thank you for your love, example-ship, and guidance, even when I may not like it.

Happy Father's Day.
Your son,
Jacob Leavitt
2013

FINANCIAL RUIN

MYRON AND I HAVE NOT had a perfect marriage, and we certainly have some memories that we would love a "do-over" for if we could. Times when we've blown our top in anger or allowed relational cracks to widen to chasms. Or times when we've chosen to believe the worst in the other instead of giving the benefit of the doubt. We've also deeply wounded each other—with words or actions we regret.

Sometimes I forget that even though Myron is strong, there's a tender heart inside. And when I sling verbal accusations, though he may appear stoic, I've wounded him in ways that cause distance, not the connection that I'm craving.

On top of that, I have a bad tendency to be so busy with my own life that sometimes I fail to see the needs of those around me. It's not that I don't care about them. If I'm brutally honest, I guess I just care about myself more. Until something jarring awakens me out of the self-absorbed world I'm in, that is.

One day in 2004 I was in the kitchen working on dinner and I knew Myron was on the phone with his boss, but I was only half-listening until I heard him say, "Jenny, come here, please."

As I rounded the corner, the sight brought me up short. Before me sat my husband, looking broken and as if the weight of the world rested on his shoulders.

"That was my boss. I can't go back to work. They're sending me home on workman's comp full time. I don't know what we're going to do."

Myron had broken his back when he fell off the top of a thirty-foot ladder while at work. He'd already taken a reduction in work hours and been moved to light duty. For a man who has an ingrained work ethic and is a firm believer in providing for his family, this last blow was almost too much to bear.

I stood there for a minute, thinking, and weighing my words carefully. I only half-joked when I say that I'm a little slow on the uptake. I'm the one who thinks of the "perfect" response—a day later.

Myron was trying to explain my delayed response time to some friends once when he said, "Our family was driving along, and she was sitting up front in the passenger seat, and both the boys were sitting in the back. There was a dog in the back of a truck right next to us barking his head off. We got up to a traffic light and my wife goes, 'Oh, a dog.' It had been there for thirty minutes. *Barking*. We'd been beside it for thirty minutes."

Our friend laughed and said, "I bet road trips are very entertaining."

To which Myron replied with yet another story, "When I met Jenny, she had this little red pickup, and one of the blinkers was blinking faster than the other one. I kept telling her that she needed to check the blinker fluid. I kept asking her, 'Didn't your dad check the blinker fluid yet?'

"'No. Ugh. I keep forgetting,' she would say.

"I'd say, 'You've got to talk to your dad. Have him check the blinker fluid. You're going to get in a wreck if you don't.' This went on for at least a year. At least a *year*. You know what I found her last Christmas?"

"No, what did you find her?" our friends asked.

"A little bottle of blinker fluid. She really appreciated it."

I felt compelled to chime in with, "Guys, we've been married twenty-seven years, and I have not lived that down. Both of our boys weren't even alive then and they know the blinker fluid story."

Myron continued, "She'd probably still think there's blinker fluid if a buddy of mine hadn't been like, 'Blinker fluid? What are you talking about?'"

My clumsiness and lack of observational skills have been a running joke in our family for quite some time. I've often told people that you better have a thick skin to be in the Leavitt family . . . or be willing to develop one.

One of the advantages of this quirk is that *generally*, since I'm slow in responding, I think before I speak. Not always, mind you. But that day, when I saw my husband looking so defeated, I knew that whatever I said *at that moment* would be crucial, not only for Myron, but for our relationship and our family's future.

I wanted him to know that just like he was there for me during the cancer, I would be there for him during this trial too.

An internal dialogue began as I thought, *Well, that's good that you want to encourage him, but really. What can you say to help?*

I remembered all the times that God was faithful to us in the past and I knew that he'd be faithful now.

Then I knew what I needed to say.

"Myron, can I pray for you? God's going to help you. And us."

Lifting his head to meet my eyes, he said, "Yeah. You can."

The gratitude on his face was almost palpable. I don't remember what I prayed exactly. I just know that I wanted to convey my love and support to Myron while reminding both of us that somehow God would bring his promise to pass that "in all things God works for the good of those who love him, who have been called according to his purpose."

Another GodPrint moment that I would look back on in the days to come—a time when Myron and I chose once again to trust, despite the grave circumstances we were in.

WHEN THE BOTTOM
FALLS OUT

WE LOST IT ALL WHILE Myron waited over a year for back surgery.

Two houses, cars, furniture—all of it, gone.

In the middle of all of that, his dad was put into hospice care, and we were told he didn't have much longer to live. We had to sell almost everything else we had to raise the money to fly out to Idaho for Christmas that year to be with family.

Myron said one time to our little church, "Here I was, supposed to be the provider for my family, and unable to work. There was this fear that the money will run out and not cover all of the bills. This fear of not providing and that when times are tight, the money and resources won't be there. That giant of fear daunted me. I had to name the giant of defeat and decide: Do I have more faith in this giant than I do in God? The Bible says that God, who created the universe, has called us by name and knows the number of hairs on our head. So, when that fear rises up, we can say, 'I am God's. I do not belong to fear, nor do I have to live in fear any longer.'"

Honestly, we'd have to be dead to not feel some fear when the bottom falls out, but one GodPrint God left on our hearts through my cancer ordeal was that he is faithful. He provided for us when Myron was laid off from his job a week after my treatments started. He supernaturally provided a way for Myron to take care of our young family and be there for me at the same time.

We had to hold onto those reference points when we were forced to short sell our home and move into a pay-by-the-week hotel for two months while we searched for a place to live. I was able to pick up more hours at work to help out. Myron picked up some odd jobs trying to make ends meet. Ever feel like you might finally get your ends to meet and then somebody just moves the ends?

Then Myron met a guy who owned a beat-up, rundown double-wide trailer out in the country. The place had been destroyed by the last tenants. There were holes in the walls the size of a man, the house reeked of urine, and the entire thing had to be renovated. Myron worked out a deal with him that we would do the work and he would reduce the rent each month. The agreement was that after the seven-month lease ended, we would buy it.

To save money, we went ahead and moved from the hotel into the trailer just as soon as the holes were patched and the home could be secured. Then all four of us went to work to renovate the place. I say all four of us, but really Myron took the brunt of the work because the boys and I didn't have much construction experience. Thank God for brothers and sisters in the church that came out to help us when they could too. The house was really turning into a pretty place by the time his surgery was finally scheduled.

In the meantime, we still found simple and cheap things to do as a family. There's nothing quite like a cold popsicle on a hot Florida summer day or sitting on the couch with the boys catching up on our reading time together. One of the benefits of reading together was being able to teach them to look at what's really being said in the story. Does it line up with what we know Scripture says? If not, is it something that we really should be putting into our minds?

I remember one time being so proud of Caleb when he came home from school and casually commented in conversation that he returned a book to the school library because he kept reading parts that were very questionable. He said that he decided that it just was not what he should be reading. My heart leapt with joy—*he got it*. He understood what I'd been trying to teach them.

When the weather cooled off some, the boys and I loved to go for walks around the neighborhood, talking about our day. Trips to the park were a highlight too.

The trailer that we moved into was about a half-hour drive from the church, so we had lots of travel time to spend together every week. We've always been faithful to both services on Sunday and church on Wednesday night. On top of that, we volunteer in a lot of different ministries, so we had a lot of time in the car. We talked about serious topics like heaven and hell, but also just frivolous, elementary-age boy stuff too.

The library was another favorite place of ours, and one of our favorite things to check out were books on tape. To this day, we still sometimes tease Caleb that he is Hank the Cowdog. In the audio series we listened to, Hank was constantly checking the perimeters of his property to make sure everything was secure. In the same way, Caleb was always the one to make sure all of the doors were locked and everything was secure before we went to bed at night.

Once we got settled into the trailer, we added a basset hound named Sherman to our family. Sherman was entertaining all by himself, but he was so stupid. He would get loose and just go lay out in the middle of the road sunning himself until he got hit by a car. Thankfully the vet was able to intervene, and Sherman recovered. But do you think he learned? Oh no. He went right back out to the road and took a nap in the middle of the street.

When I look back on that time in our life though, some of my favorite memories are of fellowshipping with our brothers and sisters in Christ that would come out to help us. We've always been the type of family that loved to have people over for a good meal, play some games, toss a football.

After we got the place all fixed up, some good friends brought over some fresh fish they had caught along with the supplies to make cheese grits. Being a southern-raised girl, I've had cheese grits before, but I had never tried them with seafood. Boy, was I missing out! Ever since that day, our family loves shrimp and cheese grits.

Myron was telling one of our church members about that time of testing when finances were the tightest they've ever been and said, "It was not easy to trust God when I broke my back while working. That was a storm that was too big for me to carry. For God, it was nothing but an opportunity to show me who he is."

It always makes us chuckle when people tell us about their money problems and then look at us and say something like, "You just don't understand what it's like."

Oh yes we do. Just because we didn't stay in that broke state does not mean we have always been financially stable.

Believe it or not, I count this experience as a GodPrint. What the world says should be humiliating—losing all of our material possessions—was just another reminder that there's so much more to life than *things*. People are so much more important. Relationships, friendships that endure—those are worth more than all the gold on planet earth. We don't walk this path alone, but have joined the family of God and can find encouragement in that.

I will admit, though, that I never shared with anybody at my job about us living out of a hotel. I can't stand pity, and more than anything, I didn't want any handouts. It was probably just my pride—not wanting anyone to know we were homeless.

In one of Myron's sermons on trusting God he said, "It's easy to trust Jesus when you can see him moving. It's much different trusting him in the storms of life when you can't see him. You still have to go back and say, 'Jesus, I trust you whether I understand it or not.'"

Myron could preach a sermon like that with confidence because our confidence with God's ability grew with each trial that he brought us through. We found him to be faithful in using every hardship to strengthen our faith and remind of us our dependency on him. We found him to be real and alive and very much concerned with the intimate details of his children's lives.

We didn't realize that at the time, but everything we had been through was to help prepare us for the greatest battle of our lives in a few short years.

Dear Dad,

As I continue to grow older, both physically and spiritually, it becomes more and more obvious that I resemble you in innumerable ways. To be honest, in my past teenage years, when people would say I was "just like you," I would hate it. I wanted to be my own person, unique from everyone else, not "just like" anyone. And yet, I have begun to realize that we must all be like someone else, that we will all mimic and follow a certain person or people. It is a simple fact of life, and while I realize you are not perfect, just as every other human is not, I also realize that if I followed your example, I would be a hard-working, God-loving, stubborn, and caring man, and I truly desire these God-given traits. I'm not really good with this emotional stuff, but I love you Dad and know that you love me too. Forgive me for my selfishness and non-caring attitude. You truly are a gift to my life and your care for my destiny in Christ is obvious. I just hope that my life and decisions will make you proud to call me your son.

Love,
Caleb
2013

WHAT MATTERS MOST

I HATE HOSPITALS. THEY EVOKE such bad memories for me. The sickly smell of death and decay covered with strong antiseptic. The freezing cold temperatures and the endless hours of waiting.

It was different this time, though, since I was the one in the waiting room and Myron was the one in surgery. Sitting there in the waiting area, my mind bounced back to all the times I had to wait to be called for a follow-up chest X-ray to make sure everything was still clear. I remember the first time a technician asked me if I had a pacemaker.

"Um, no, I do not have a pacemaker. Why?"

"Oh, well, there appears to be a small metal device or something near or in your heart."

Come to find out, when they'd biopsied the lymph node near my heart, somehow a small clamp was left inside of me. I have been assured that it is doing no damage and would actually cause more problems if they went in to remove it now. So even all these years later, I have a clamp near my heart that shows up on every chest X-ray.

Even though these memories of hospital waiting rooms were not pleasant, my anxiety this time was over my husband. He had been trying to make light of the impending surgery by joking around about how sad it was that this was the first time the Super Bowl came to Jacksonville, and even though he was less than a mile away from the stadium in the hospital, he may as well have been a thousand miles away.

All jokes aside, when the doctor came out to me in the waiting room when he finished the surgery, he explained to me just how bad Myron's back injury was by comparing it to a jelly-filled donut. He said that Myron's vertebrae had collapsed so profoundly that all of the jelly had been squirted out and there was no way to put it back in. He fused everything back together the best he could, but warned that the damage was severe.

When I was allowed to go back and see Myron, it tore at my heart as I stood over him as he was moaning in pain. My strong husband who never complains about physical pain was asking for pain medicines. It scared me.

What scared me even more, though, was that right after Myron had back surgery, he went right back to working on that trailer. It was driving him nuts to not be able to provide a suitable place for his family to live and feel safe. I remember standing off to the side while he worked on the kitchen just days after his surgery, pleading with him to just take it easy.

Myron and I have had our fair share of disagreements over the years, and that was definitely one of them. To make a long story short, Myron recovered, we worked hard, and the place looked amazing when we were done.

A month before the lease ended, the landlord called to say he was selling the trailer and that we needed to move out.

"What happened to us buying it? We did all this work and that was the agreement," Myron said.

"I'm selling it. If you can buy it next month, I'll sell it to you. If not, you need to move out."

Legally, we had no recourse since we had nothing in writing. It was our word against his. So, once again, we were homeless.

I'll be honest with you—we had to really pray and ask God to help us to forgive him and to process the entire situation.

With such short notice and with Myron still not released to go back to work, we struggled to find a place to live. A friend of ours from church had a large mobile home and offered to let us live with her and her two sons. Caleb and Jacob loved the idea because they were good friends with her boys and thought it would be awesome to live with them. We transferred most of our stuff into storage and moved in with them.

Three weeks later, her landlord said, "All of you need to move out."

No warning. Just, "Move out."

Once again, we were homeless. Back to the pay-by-the-week hotel we went. This time we stayed a little longer because I told Myron that I'd rather stay there until we could find a place of our own to rent so that the next time we moved, we'd be staying put for a while.

In the meantime, we decided we were going to make the best of it. I still remember that for Christmas that year, we decided as a family to focus on others. We couldn't have a tree or anything in the hotel room, so we went to the store together as a family and purchased gifts and food for some families in the church who were struggling. We all piled in the car, snuck up to their front door, and left it on their porch. It was so much fun.

That was also the first year that we participated in the Operation Christmas Child campaign that Samaritan's Purse coordinates each year. We had a blast going to the dollar store and picking out all kinds of little things to include in the shoebox that would be sent across the world to a child who had nothing. That put our own situation into perspective and made us grateful all over again for what we had.

I had transferred jobs to a school that was less than a mile from the trailer we were in out in the country because we thought we were purchasing the mobile home. To be able to afford the rent on a house now, we had to move back into town, about a thirty-minute drive away.

The house that we eventually rented was in a rough neighborhood. Seriously, the boys and I witnessed a drug deal at the neighborhood park one time. Another time, a guy who had stolen food from the grocery store behind our house hopped the back fence while fleeing the police. He ran through our backyard to the front, chucking food out of his pants while the boys were tossing the football with some neighbor kids.

I can't tell you how many times helicopter search lights would shine through our bedroom window at night.

Once again, we decided to make the best of it, and the boys and I started using the travel time in the mornings to read in a children's devotional and pray together. This was one way that we tried to be intentional with our parenting and use the time that we had. It still warms my heart to think back on some of those conversations we had as a result of the devotional topics. It's not an exaggeration to say that I am eternally grateful now for those talks.

Myron often uses this time of our lives to illustrate that we can never outgive God. Even through all of those financially difficult years, we never stopped tithing or giving to God, and he never once failed us. We always had a roof over our heads—even if it was a hotel. We never went hungry. We had plenty of clothes and all the necessities.

More importantly, though, we had each other. We were all healthy and whole. We had great friends, loving family, and joy that was rooted in knowing who we are in Christ. Not the temporary happiness the world offers, but deep, abiding joy and peace from God.

You told me how to be forgiven from my sin,
And you have helped through the thick and thin.
Even when you lost your job and Grandad died,
You never were once dissatisfied.
You loved God the whole time,
And that is why I have wrote this rhyme.
Thank you, Dad, for showing me to always trust in God.
—Portion of handmade birthday card from
Caleb to Myron 2007

MOVING UP

WE STAYED IN THAT RENTED house for two and-a-half years while Myron finished recovering, went back to work, and we rebuilt our financial stability. It was in that house that we moved a young new convert to Christ in with us. Over the years we've had a lot of people live with us while they got back on their feet or established a foundation in their Christianity.

This young man really hit it off with our boys and introduced them to Christian rap music. He is a big reason why sometimes I listened to rap music on those long car rides even when I didn't feel like it. I guess I didn't really have to. But the lyrics were God-honoring, and my boys loved it, so why would I not want to encourage them to fill their minds with godly things instead of foul, worldly rap? I love music, and there are several Christian rap artists that I enjoy to this day.

In the middle of all this, some of the long-term side effects of the cancer treatments began popping up. From 2012 to 2015 I had one surgery each year. Every single one of them was in some way related to the radiation. I had been healthy for so many years that these issues really brought home the reminder again that I had been given a second chance at life.

Like I told Jacob, they didn't have many options for me back then. I may have to deal with the long-term side effects, but at least I was still alive.

As we got our financial footing again, we were able to buy another house out in the country. When we had first moved to the condemned trailer, this city girl had a hard time adjusting to country life. After a while, though, I grew to absolutely love the wide-open spaces and the ability to see the stars at night. I loved to see deer feeding on the roadside on the way home from church at night or to go for peaceful walks down winding country lanes.

In our new home, back out in the country, we were able to enjoy all of that and more. We now had plenty of room to plant several gardens—vegetable and flower—and host pool parties in our backyard.

The boys grew from those rambunctious boys to rowdy teenagers in that house. I think their friends had a love/hate feeling about coming over to our house on the weekends. They knew that they were always welcome and there was always fun to be had. But they also knew that whatever the boys were going to be doing, they'd be roped into as well. Washing and vacuuming the car? Yep, they could help with that. Weeding the four raised garden beds? Oh yes, they absolutely could help with that. Pick up trash along the little stretch of dirt road leading from the stop sign to our driveway? Here's some gloves and a trash bag. I'll have a cold popsicle or some watermelon waiting for you when you're finished.

Some of my fondest memories of those days are of watching those young teens toss the football outside or hearing their loud laughter as they played a game.

We'd enjoy a swim in the pool after working outside together or feeding the crew after one project or another. We weren't the only ones who lived thirty minutes from the church, so we also carpooled for youth events too. Sometimes I'd be toting home five or six teenagers that were stirred up from the night's youth-ministry event. I would just be driving and listening like a fly on the wall while they excitedly talked about it all.

Occasionally somebody would cross a line and I would think, *I'm the adult in the car. I need to bring a balance to this.* Most of the time it was just lighthearted stuff, but sometimes they would say something that needed to be addressed, and I would have a "teachable moment" with them.

Caleb and Jacob would just groan and say something like, "Mom, why do you have to take everything to the serious level and go so deep?"

"Because I'm a mom and I can't just let that one go by without commenting."

Remember that accident I mentioned that Jacob felt so guilty about? It happened one cool, spring Florida morning in 2013. When Jacob knocked on my bedroom door, I instantly knew he missed the bus. Doing my best to restrain the frustration, the detour delayed me enough to throw off my morning routine and cause me to run late to work.

After I dropped Jacob off at the high school, I merged back into the traffic creeping down the busy highway. As I sat at the red light, a glance in the rearview mirror brought a burst of panic. Before I could even finish the thought, *Hm . . . that truck is coming awfully fast. It's not going to be able—*

SLAM!

Loud screeching, glass shattering, and my Expedition went lunging forward through the intersection.

I barely had enough time to jerk the steering wheel into the median and avoid crashing into the back of the vehicle on the *other side* of the intersection.

The impact was so violent, so sudden, that it totaled my vehicle, sending the third-row seating into the second row. The driver's seat was so jarred by the impact that when the vehicle came to a stop, I was laying back at a contorted angle. The first person to open my door *just happened* to be an off-duty EMT who stayed with me until help arrived.

Long story short, it was a long road of recovery from the neck and shoulder injuries I sustained. On top of the long-term cancer treatment issues that were cropping up, now I had to deal with a torn labrum and rotator cuff from the seat belt. Eventually I had to have surgery to have them repaired followed by months of physical therapy.

I also had severe injuries to my neck—almost all of the vertebrae were blown except for the very top one that attached to the brain stem.

Our tender-hearted Jacob felt horrible when he found out about the accident after school that day. He apologized over and over for missing the bus, feeling that he was responsible for me being in the area later than normal.

"Jacob," I told him, "don't do that to yourself. Do you think God was sleeping? Do you think he was unaware of what was going on? No. He knew and he was with me. It could have been a lot worse."

His face brightened a little, but he still battled with guilt over his part in the timing.

The neck injury caused incredible headaches too, which led me to a neurologist's office. At that point, I was experiencing pain and numbness in the left side of my face. Even the left side of my tongue would go numb for periods of time. I was shocked to hear the doctor casually say that I probably had some nerve necropsy going on.

I don't have a medical degree, but I know necropsy refers to death of some kind.

I asked, "Um, what exactly does nerve necropsy mean?"

He said, "Oh, it means that you probably have some nerves in your face and jaw that have died. But we wouldn't know for sure unless we did an autopsy. Which we obviously won't do right now."

I would hope not.

The road of Christianity will always lead you
through the things, not above or around them.
—Jacob Leavitt's personal notes from Pastor Ron Meyer's
sermon "This Mountain" (10/23/2013)

MOVING FORWARD

WE WERE IN THAT HOUSE eleven years.

During that time Myron started his own successful side business. It became like a two-edged sword for me. While I was so proud of him, there was also a lot of tension between us about how much time he spent away from the family. Between church commitments, his full-time day job, and his side business, there were lots of days when I saw very little of him.

This is one of the areas of our marriage where I wish I had a do-over. I wish I had approached those discussions in a better way. It's hard when you have not had an example of that in your life. How can you live something you've never known? How can you pass on what you haven't learned yet yourself?

I have learned since then how that mindset in itself can become a crutch in my life. It's way too easy to throw up my hands and say, "See, I just don't know how to communicate," while I surrender hopes and dreams for true intimacy with my husband. Because honestly, that's easier than putting in the work necessary to learn how to communicate better. Proverbs 18:2 says, "A fool takes no pleasure in understanding, but only in expressing his opinion."

Ouch.

But as Myron has said many times before, "We can't change the past. We just have to learn from it and move forward."

This was also a season in our lives when we didn't exactly make our physical health a priority—all of us put on weight. In an effort to get that under control, Jacob and I began getting up before school every morning and going for a walk. At the end of our walk, we would take the last half mile or so and pray together just like we used to do when we would drive together to school in the mornings. I learned so much about Jacob's heart through that time of prayer, especially his heart for his generation and wanting to see revival in his peers.

We'd also pray for God's protection over our family, along with asking God to give us each wisdom as we went about our day and for opportunities to share our faith with those around us.

By that time, Jacob was six feet tall and over 300 pounds—But, oh, he was a big teddy bear on the inside. Always a peacemaker, he'd be the one to step in when tensions were mounting and try to cool things off. Sometimes with a joke. Sometimes a well-worded point of reason.

One time, the four of us were in the living room discussing the family "homework" for Sunday school that week. Each of us was to share one good thing about the other. In this discussion, the meaning of each of the boys' names came up. Caleb has heard the story of his name all his life, and it's been quite interesting to see just how accurate Caleb's "warrior" name proved to be over the years.

We also discussed how Jacob's biblical namesake, also known as Israel in the Bible, was the second son just like our Jacob. Jacob/Israel had issues (don't we all?) that plagued him all his life. Those issues finally came to a head when he wrestled all night with God, refusing to give up until God blessed him. God touched him, forever changing him in a moment.

In the living room that night, I told our Jacob that my prayer for him was that he would experience his own "wrestling with God until breakthrough" experience. In hindsight, I had no idea what I was asking.

One of the most rewarding things that Myron and I have ever done had been working with the youth of our church. Sometimes we'll look around at the worship team, the drama team, nursery workers, cleanup crew—any of them serving behind the scenes— and gratitude will fill our hearts. It's amazing to know that we had a small part in helping to ignite these young people's hearts for Jesus as we partnered with their parents to teach them God's ways. What a privilege to show the next generation that there is hope and that God does love them intimately and wants to be a part of their day-to-day lives.

The summer of 2015, God had been stirring Jacob's heart to contend for his peers' salvation. His youth group, Lifeline, came back fired up for Jesus after a weeklong summer camp designed specially to help teenagers meet a living Savior and then go home and impact their world.

One of our greatest treasures is a video we have of Jacob testifying with some of his peers in church service the Sunday night after their return.

In typical Jacob fashion, he began with a joke, "First of all, I want to say that I'm not wearing my shirt because I'm rebellious. I'm not wearing it because it made me look like a sausage casing."

After the laughter died down, he quickly became serious as he continued, "And secondly, I just want to thank you guys for supporting us teenagers because there's no price tag you could put on seeing all these lives changed. There's nothing you could sell, buy, or compare to all the lives saved that are going to come out of this group. Really, one of the things that God hammered into my heart this past week was that religiosity will lead to you being bitter. It will lead to all these different things that cause you to eventually backslide.

"Growing up in church we get in a routine of coming, raising our hands but keeping one eye wide open to see if Pastor's watching. On Wednesday night, our youth pastor preached on motivation, money, and morality. He gave us these keys to success, but at the end he said, 'All these keys aren't going to work unless you have Jesus, because your life means nothing without Jesus.'

". . . One more thing. If I can say anything to you guys, it's please don't give up on this generation. Because we're here with lights in our hearts. A light that can't be dimmed by anything that will ever happen."

Who, but God, could have known what was coming in a few short weeks?

Who, but God, could have known that those challenging words would become Jacob's legacy?

Who, but God, could have prepared Jacob, and us, ahead of time in so many ways like this for the events that would separate our lives into *before* and *after*?

God *did* know, though. And he *did* prepare us.

This video—all of it—is a GodPrint.

We just didn't know it or see it at the time.

Sometimes it's too easy to take for granted the simple days of life. For the daily routine to become just that—routine.

Too easy for marriages to drift apart. To wake up one day and realize that it's been a long time since you felt that closeness, that real intimacy that once defined the relationship.

Too easy to let days go by without connecting with your kids.

Until something earth-shattering happens, and you wish with everything within you that you could to return to those mundane, routine days.

But you can't. Because like it or not, life goes on.

The main thing that I took out of this was to get out of my religious comfort zone. Growing up in church, it becomes easy to get familiar with the things of God. Really living for him requires us to break out of the norm and be willing to do what God asks of us. Gideon may have been weak, but through God's power, he broke out of his lifelong routine and saved his entire nation.
—Handwritten note in Jacob Leavitt's
Summer Camp Booklet July 2015

Every Parent's Worst Nightmare

AUGUST 29, 2015, WAS ANOTHER pivotal day in my life. *Our* lives.

Really, it was the day that changed our family storyline forever. To *before* and *after*.

The shrill ring of Myron's cellphone piercing through the night should've been a warning of what was coming. With my history of receiving bad news through phone calls, I should have suspected something was awry.

As we stepped into the house and Myron reached for the living room light switch, though, I was still blissfully unaware of the chaos unfolding twenty miles away.

"Myron, do you know where your boys are at?" our pastor's wife asked when he answered.

"Well, they're either at church or they're on their way home."

He was pretty confident they were, anyway. We'd all been at

our church for a special event that Saturday night. It was almost midnight because, as usual, we were some of the first to arrive and the last to leave. The event was very successful and even though we were tired, it was worth all the effort.

She continued, "We were driving down the highway and came across a wreck. It looked like your son's truck was involved."

Myron told me later that he thought to himself, *There are a lot of little red Ford Escapes around.* So, okay, no big deal.

He responded, "I'll give them a call and check on them. I'll let you know."

There was a moment of silence and then she said, "I don't want to scare you, but the truck is on fire."

Oh, wow.

"Okay, I'll call and see if everyone's all right. Thanks."

We tried calling and texting both of our sons and neither one answered, which was odd for them. We knew if one of them was driving the other would've answered.

Myron could tell that I was concerned. After all, we'd just walked in the door, and it was unusual to get a phone call that late at night. Unbeknownst to me at the time, even though Myron didn't think it could possibly be our son's truck, just *in case* it was, he wanted to spare me as much as possible until he knew what we were up against.

Turning to me, he said, "Hey, babe, why don't you stay here so that when they get home, you can let me know? I'm going to start heading toward the accident and just check it out. I'm sure they're fine and it's not them."

The accident location was about twenty minutes away from our house, but just a few minutes away from the church. As Myron was heading that way, more friends who had left the event after us called to tell him, "The entire road is blocked off by emergency vehicles. We were able to go around a back way and get to the accident. You need to know, it's definitely Caleb's truck."

They wouldn't tell him anything other than that: *It's definitely Caleb's truck.*

His mind scrambled to catch up with this as he told them, "Okay, I'm two minutes away."

Our boys were in an accident. One so bad that an entire four-lane highway was shut down.

Myron drove through the drizzling rain around the back as they suggested. As he rounded the bend, the normally dark intersection was lit up with flashing red, white, and blue—firetrucks, ambulances, police cruisers, state troopers.

He remembers thinking, *This does not look good.*

Glass crunched under his feet as he walked across the four-lane highway. A quick scan of the area showed debris everywhere. Scattered glass mixed with twisted metal from one end to the other haphazardly. Even the median and tree line was covered in vehicle parts. Random, broken objects that were thrown out of the vehicles upon impact littered the area. Papers and trash swirled in the mist right alongside shredded pieces of rubber and headlights.

He could see a large Chevy pickup truck down the road just a little bit, up in the woods. It was a gnarled mess. When he saw that vehicle, his first thought was, *Somebody in that truck died.*

He looked for the closest police officer he could find, desperate for any information on our boys, but also concerned about whoever was in that pickup truck. We later learned that the two eighteen-year-old boys in that vehicle were recent high school graduates out for a night of partying and joy riding. They found someone willing to provide them with a large amount of alcohol and then decided to get behind the wheel and try to make it home.

Surprisingly, neither one of them died that night. The driver's blood alcohol content was .22 when they took a blood draw several hours later. The legal limit for someone over twenty-one years old in Florida is .08.

So when he blew through the intersection, going sixty-nine

miles per hour and t-boned our twenty-year-old son's SUV, he was completely inebriated.

The second vehicle he came across was every parent's worst nightmare.

It was Caleb's Ford Escape.

As Myron grappled with his fear and uncertainty and raced to the scene, I paced and prayed. Back and forth, back and forth, across the kitchen floor. Worry, fear, and anxiety battling faith, hope, and peace.

The reality of the situation still had not set in. I've learned since that in God's great mercy, there's a stage of grief that many recognize as "fog." It envelopes you when you receive alarming news, absorbing some of the blunt pain that would otherwise overwhelm you if you were to grasp the startling reality all at once.

Surely, *surely* there was a mistake. This must be someone else.

I tried calling Myron—no answer.

I tried texting and calling both boys. No response.

I called the police department. Yes, there was a crash. But no red Ford Escape was involved.

So much confusion. So much misinformation.

Should I go to the scene? Should I stay here in case they come home? What should I do?

Finally, I said, "Enough!"

"Oh, God—all those years ago, you said you loved my boys even more than I do. Even though that's hard for me to fathom because I love them so much, you said it. I believe it. You said you'd take care of them, and I trust you to do that. No matter what happens, I trust you. Even if it is our boys, I trust you."

A faith that cannot be tested is a faith that cannot be trusted.
—Pastor Ron Meyer (handwritten note in Jacob Leavitt's Bible)

17

WHAT'S GOING ON?

EVEN IN THE CHAOS OF the accident scene, Myron could see that the front end of Caleb's Ford Escape was almost entirely cleaved off by the force of the impact. The remaining part was smoldering from the fire. Rescue personnel and state troopers were securing the area.

He ran across the road yelling, "Where are my sons?"

In the confusion, he was told that our son had been taken to the trauma hospital in downtown Jacksonville.

"I have two sons. They were both in the vehicle."

"No, sir. Only one person from that vehicle was taken to the hospital. You should go there as soon as possible."

He thought, *Is it possible that Jacob rode home with someone else? But why would he have done that? He wouldn't have changed his plans without talking to us first. One of them would have called us.*

The officers were adamant that only one of our sons was there. Only one of our sons was taken to the ER. They began to physically remove him from the site, pushing him off to the side of the road. He didn't realize it at the time, but it was an active crime scene involving a drunk driver and a fatality.

As if in slow motion, he turned around and saw beyond the Escape. . . .

Beyond the engine that was on one side of the road while the truck body was on the other side. . . .

Beyond the debris littering the roadway, the median, even the shoulder. . . .

Beyond the twisted metal in the grass and trees. . . .

He wondered why he hadn't seen it before.

Had he seen it, but his mind didn't want to register what he was witnessing?

Like I said, our son Jacob was a big boy. You couldn't miss him. There, on the roadway, was a body covered in a white sheet.

A large body.

He shouted, "That's my son!"

As he tried to run toward Jacob, an officer restrained him, saying, "What? No sir, that's not your son. Your son's on the way to the hospital. You need to go there. Now."

The officer didn't tell Myron that Caleb was in critical condition and was fighting for his life. He just continued to urgently tell him to go . . . *Now*.

Our good friend and assistant pastor, Jeremy, was there with him. This was the same friend who knocked on my door with Myron when I was a sixteen-year-old girl and invited me out to the little concert in my neighborhood. This was the same man who was a walking medical miracle of God's healing power.

Together, they tried pleading with the officers to let them near Jacob. "Can we just go over and pray for him?"

Jeremy told the officer, "I was hit by a drunk driver when I was eleven years old, and my dad came and prayed for me and I'm alive today. Can we please go pray for him?"

The officer firmly replied, "Absolutely not. It's a crime scene. You cannot go in there."

Myron has said, with tears in his eyes and a gravelly voice, "I wish I could explain to you what it is like to turn and see your youngest son laying in the middle of a wet highway, dead. If you could, you would go and hug every loved one you have. And you would certainly never get behind the wheel of a vehicle drunk."

Do you know how people say that when you're dying, scenes of your life flash through your mind? Well, standing there in that moment, realizing that Jacob was under that sheet, hell assaulted Myron's mind. But for him, what played back in his mind was all the missed opportunities. All the times he could've been there and wasn't. Times when he was a little too stern, a little too rough. The guilt hit him in such a powerful way that he literally grabbed his head and doubled over to his knees on the asphalt.

Holding his head in his hands, image after image fired through his brain. All the times in Jacob's life when he had been too harsh or too judgmental. All the mistakes he made as a father, and his absolute inability to do anything about it now. Wave after wave of guilt, until he didn't know if he could survive it.

He thought he would crumble under the weight of the guilt, but by God's mercy, he didn't. He says he can only attribute it to God holding him together, helping him stand back up.

Even as our seventeen-year-old son, who had just finished the second week of his senior year of high school, was on the road, covered with a sheet.

Guilt knows that it deserves punishment,
but Jesus' blood was the atonement.
—Pastor Roman Gutierrez (handwritten note
in Jacob Leavitt's Bible, April 27, 2015)

18

THE LONGEST NIGHT

MYRON'S PROTECTIVE INSTINCT KICKED IN. He asked Jeremy's wife Tiffany to drive out to our house, pick me up, and drive me to the hospital. He was trying to shield me from the blunt, graphic reality he'd already witnessed.

Tiffany purposely avoided driving us the most direct route, as that would take us right past the intersection. Even then, we were still only a half mile from the crash site. I turned my head to the right as we passed by the intersection and the scene came into view. Thank God we were traveling by too fast and too far away to see details. Unfortunately, I saw enough to burn the image into my psyche forever.

Through the mist, a spirit of fear—terror—swept across me. The hard slap of reality said, *This is really happening. We are really facing this. Not someone else. Us. The Leavitts.*

The intensive care waiting room was as cold as a meat locker. Only a hard plastic loveseat, side table, and chair would fit in the tiny space. The bleak, bland walls were sterile, devoid of art or signs of life. That antiseptic hospital smell along with an air of hopelessness permeated the room. Hours of just sitting and waiting, the finality of death lingered so close you could feel it in your bones.

Myron and I sat there, huddled together, sifting through the onslaught of crushing fear and uncertainty. Waiting, waiting, waiting.

Where's Jacob? Why can't they tell us anything about him? Why are they saying that they only have one of our sons here? That they have no record of a Jacob Leavitt at the hospital?

Will Caleb survive? How bad is he? Why won't they let us see him?

What happened? Why can't we get straight answers? When will they come back with an update?

Will our marriage survive this? Will our family survive this?

In the hospital lobby, over a hundred of our church friends and family crowded together in prayer and support. Hospital staff repeatedly commented on how impressed they were by the church's care for us and their respect for the hospital staff. "The love for the brethren" our dear friends exuded as they labored in prayer for us and our boys was a touchpoint of stability when we couldn't even think straight—a precious, life-giving GodPrint.

The door opened.

State troopers walked in.

My eyes flickered to the bag in one of their hands.

No. No. No.

The bag held nineteen dollars and eleven cents, eye drops, and a bloody class ring.

They finally figured out where Jacob was. He hadn't been taken to the hospital.

He'd been taken to the morgue.

Our youngest son was dead at seventeen.

Would we lose Caleb too?

Oh, God.

Please, no—we can't lose them both in one night.

Lord, . . . you've been so merciful and kind to me—compassionate in my failings, compassionate in my grief, speaking to the depths of my heart and hearing every bit of torment, of anguish—every cry from my heart. You are so good, walking with me, right here, right now. Being life when it feels dead. Being hope when it's hard to see any. Being joy, deep down inside of me—that because of you, because of your amazing plan—your life, your atoning death, your glorious resurrection—I can have hope and joy. ONE DAY, because of you alone, I will see my precious Jacob again. I will wrap my arms around him and smother him with my love . . . I'll tell him, "Oh, how I've missed you, dear son." And on that day, I will spend the rest of forever with him, not just merely another seventeen years. Oh, for the longing. To be in your perfect place for eternity, Lord—the place you have prepared for those who love you.

Sometimes I feel so selfish and not patient at all—wanting so badly for you to come, Jesus. To abolish death, hell, and the grave forever. For you, faithful and true King Jesus, to reign victorious. And because of your great victory, for me to be healed of this heartache and to embrace my precious son again. Come soon, Lord Jesus.

~From Jenny's private journal

DID GOD REALLY SAY?

MYRON SLIPPED AN ARM AROUND my shoulders as we sat on that little cold loveseat, waiting for news about Caleb and talking.

"Do you think he knew I loved him?" he asked me.

"Don't do that to yourself, Myron. You were trying to raise him to be a responsible adult. A man. And a healthy one. You can't beat yourself up over that."

After more whispered words, I asked him, "Why would God heal me from cancer all those years ago, let me see him grow up, and then take him?"

At the time, neither one of us had an answer for that one.

We'd been Christians long enough to know that in this war we've been born into, the final enemy to be defeated is death. We know that Jesus already took care of that on the cross, but sometimes we get so distracted with day-to-day living that we forget the reality that death will happen to us. No one is exempt. That's why facing the untimely, tragic loss of Jacob—and others who "die before their time"—shakes us out of the denial we live in and brings us face to face with the cold, hard truth again.

When you can remember the day your child came into the world, and then you also have to face the day that you bury that same child's body in the ground, it brings the reality of death up close and personal in a way I'd never wish on anyone.

Myron has said that is when he realized that he can't change the past, but he can change how he treats people going forward. He can learn to be more like our son Jacob.

Later on, as I looked around the hospital waiting room, I was struck again at who remained to keep vigil with us. Precious sons in the faith. Friends of our boys struggling to grapple with the reality of all that had happened.

One young man, whose own mother is now waiting for us in heaven, sat with us, even as his grief was still raw and fresh.

Then there was Caleb's best friend since grade school and one of the few people who can "talk Caleb down." That friendship would prove instrumental in the days to come.

One of Jacob's best friends, who was drastically touched by Jesus at summer camp just weeks before, was there too.

Another close friend who attended Jacob's school was there too. In the time to come, he tried to honor Jacob by continuing to impact their generation with the good news about Jesus.

Some of the other younger brothers in the faith were also there. The day before the accident, they and Jacob had attended a before-school campus outreach at one of the local high schools, where they ran into one of his former classmates and shared Jesus with him.

Jacob firmly believed and prayed that his youth group would reach one hundred teens before year-end, and guess what? God heard his prayer and they had record-breaking attendance at the September Youth Rally that year. Over one hundred teens came, and many gave their lives to Christ.

Since Myron is a preacher, he shares our story with a lot of people. I remember listening one time as he said, "Have you ever noticed two people walking into an elevator talking, but once they enter the elevator, they stop talking? A few years ago, several friends and I were about to step on an elevator. The door slid open. The thing was full of people who gave us that 'hey-you-guys-aren't-gonna-try-to-get-in-are-you?' look.

"We got on.

"When my friend stepped aboard as the last one in, there wasn't room enough for him to turn around. As the door slid shut behind him, he smiled big and said loudly, 'You might have wondered why we called this meeting today.' The place broke up with laughter. It was the most amazing sight to watch. People began talking and relating to each other.

"In many respects that elevator is a picture of our world today: a large, impersonal institution where anonymity, isolation, and independence are the uniform of the day. It shows us that people can be surrounded by other people in a crowded setting, and not experience community or relationships. We can be a part of a company, a club, a school, or a church and not feel we belong or are accepted. We can share a carpool, an office, and even a home and not have significant relationships.

"We were created for relationships. We can say that we were wired to interact with other people. God planned it that way. From the beginning of time, God designed mankind to flourish in relationships. That's why God said, 'It is not good for the man to be alone' [Genesis 2:18 NIV].

"To survive in a cold and cruel world requires deep relationships. But those relationships don't just happen, they require effort. We have to do more than just reach out to others—we have to share our lives with others as well.

"Authenticity occurs when the masks come off, conversations

get deep, hearts get vulnerable, lives are shared, accountability is invited, and tenderness flows."

Just before dawn on August 30, 2015, we were reminded once again just how grateful we were for the family of God and the years of godly friendships we'd shared. Because, like it or not, it was time to tell everyone that Jacob was gone.

In the hospital lobby, that same family of God stormed heaven's gates on our behalf. They stood in the gap for us. These were our friends, our fellow brothers and sisters in Christ. Young, old, Black, White, Hispanic. Such a beautiful sea of faces. Worry etched into many of them, along with confusion.

Some of them were still in costume from the evening's special event. Others still had remnants of theatrical makeup on because they came as soon as they heard.

Caleb's friends. Jacob's friends. Precious young people we taught in children's ministry for years that God loves them, that he can be trusted, that his Word is truth and has answers for every question. We've taught them why we believe what we believe and why we do what we do. What does the Bible say about sin? Death? Heaven? Hell? Why do people fall away from the faith? What about my attitude? Does God's Word speak to everyday issues like that?

We've been teaching on these things for years. But now, with the knowledge that Jacob was gone and that Caleb was fighting for his life. . . .

Like the serpent whispered to Eve in the garden, "Has God *really* said . . . ?", the doubts tumbled through.

God, we prayed for your protection over our family almost every day. Where were you? Was it not enough?

Do I really believe all of that? I've taught it, studied it, read it, heard it.

Then, with certainty, it was settled.

Yes. Yes, I do believe it. ALL of it.

I know it's true.

Where was God?

He was right there on that roadway, meeting Jacob face to face.

Without doubt or reservation, I knew, *this is the truth.*

That moment of understanding is one of my most bittersweet, painful GodPrints to-date. But a GodPrint all the same.

*People don't need a lecture most times, they need
people who really care about them.*
—Jacob Leavitt's personal notes from Pastor Jeremy Meyer's
sermon "Flock Together" (6/19/2013)

OUR FATHER

BLOOD.

Everywhere.

Coming out of his ears, nose, and mouth. Caleb required emergency abdominal surgery to determine the cause of the internal bleeding and hopefully save his life. They'd allowed us to go back and see him, warning us how bad he was and how slim the odds of his survival were. Emotions swirled through me as we approached the gurney. Our beloved son, so full of life just a few hours ago, lay there unconscious. Bruised and broken. Swollen everywhere.

I felt a familiar sense of hopelessness as we stood there next to Caleb. That same sense that washed over me when I stood next to Myron as he was in so much pain after his first back surgery when I was helpless to do anything about it. Here was our strong son, who just like his dad plowed forward fearlessly into life's challenges, laying still and quiet as death.

We stepped right up to his side, leaning close to his ear. Desperately trying to look through eyes of faith and beyond what we were physically seeing. We reminded him that we loved him, we reassured him that we were there. Then we reminded him of who he is: a mighty warrior for God.

"It's time to fight, Caleb," I told him. "We need you to fight, son."

Right before they came to wheel him away from us, we laid our hands on Caleb and asked God for a miracle.

"God, give him the strength and will to survive."

Caleb pulled through the first surgery. The doctors came in to tell us that he survived the surgery, and they were able to stop the internal bleeding caused by a lacerated liver. They explained that he would be moved to a trauma ICU unit as soon as possible. He still had a long road of recovery ahead and wasn't completely out of the woods, but he'd made it.

Finally, a ray of hope—a root of joy in the pain of the longest night of our lives.

The warrior survived the first battle. Bruised and bloody, but alive.

Myron asked me if I wanted to go with him while he went out to update our church family in the lobby about Caleb's progress. I told him that I wanted to stay in the room just in case they came back to tell us anything else. After he left, I desperately tried to corral my thoughts into focus, but they were scattered everywhere and I had a hard time trying to latch onto even one of them, let alone string them together in a coherent prayer. In the middle of all the chaos came a memory that I grabbed onto like a drowning man grabbing a life preserver:

One of the books on tape that the boys and I listened to on those long car rides was "Let's Roll" by Lisa Beamer. After September 11, the widow of Todd Beamer from Flight 91 wrote the story of heroism that Todd and others aboard displayed as they united together to stop the terrorists who had hijacked the plane. Those heroic men and women chose to give up their lives, literally fighting to the death instead of allowing the terrorists to take even more lives.

In the book, Lisa talked about a recording of Todd on the phone with the 911 operator right before they stormed the cockpit. In the recording, Todd is heard asking the operator to pray with him. He asked her to join him in what is commonly referred to as the *Lord's Prayer*.

Lisa went on to explain how their church had been doing a Bible study that examined each segment of the famous prayer to learn the significance that Jesus was trying to impart to his followers. It was meant to be more than a rote prayer to memorize and recite. Jesus was modeling for us a meaningful way to corral our thoughts and center them on our heavenly Father who wants to hear from his children in their day-to-day lives.

Back in that sterile, cold, isolated little room off the ER, when I was alone and desperately trying to pray, I remembered that story and thought, *Okay, yes, that might help me right now.*

"Our Father . . ." Yes, God, our Father, you are my Father and I know you can hear me.

"Who art in heaven . . ." Yes, Lord. You're in heaven, you're above us and you see everything.

"Hallowed be thy name . . ." Oh God, even in all of this, hallowed be your name.

And as I went line by line, my thoughts were able to calm and my heartbeat regained somewhat of a steady rhythm. And as the tears flowed, I experienced God's reminder right there in that room. He was still in charge.

He sees. He knows.

If the devil can get a stronghold in our heart, he won't stop until he strangles the life out of us.

In our lives, the stronghold has the right to be there because we gave it jurisdiction. We can pray all that we want, but we have to revoke its charter in our lives for it to have no right.

—Jacob Leavitt's personal notes from Dad's [Myron's] sermon "Overthrowing Strongholds" (8/23/15)

SCARS

IN ALMOST THE SAME BREATH that they told us that Jacob had passed away, they told us that Caleb may be charged with vehicular homicide.

What? How is that even possible?

We already knew that the occupants of the other vehicle were wasted. While they were at the hospital, the driver was so drunk that he was fighting with the emergency room doctors and nurses. Physically fighting with them. We could hear the commotion through the closed door of the small, isolated room they tucked us in. We could even hear when the officials had to call his parents and say, "We need you to get down here right now and get him subdued or he's going to end up in handcuffs."

I remember thinking how unfair it was that some people survive drunk driving accidents and others don't. And not just the driver who walked away. I thought of our friend, Jeremy, who God granted a second chance at life after his dad prayed for him and I remember being so frustrated that the officers would not allow him and Myron to pray for Jacob. I just knew that God could have done the same for Jacob too.

I eventually found peace and reassurance from Scripture that each one of us has an allotted number of days. For whatever reason, that was Jacob's appointed time and his assignment here on earth was complete.

Obviously, God still had plans for Jeremy and for the three young men who survived the crash, Caleb included.

The state troopers explained to us that there was one witness who thought that Caleb ran the red light. If so, that would have given the oncoming truck the right-of-way.

We were gently encouraged to retain an attorney for Caleb. While he was struggling to survive his injuries, he was also facing the possibility of being charged with his own brother's death.

Myron and I had to have conversations like, "What happens if Caleb wakes up and you're not here and I have to tell him what happened? And then I have to tell him that there's a chance he could be charged with vehicular manslaughter? Or that state troopers could come in to talk to him at any point? What should I say?"

Our attorney advised us that as soon as Caleb came out of the coma and was questioned, how important it was for him to say, "I'm not answering any questions. I want a lawyer."

At that point we still had no idea what Caleb was going to be like when he came out of the coma. We knew that he had a traumatic brain injury (TBI), but we didn't know yet how bad it was. They had warned us that with this type of injury, you never know the lasting cognitive and physical changes until the person comes out of the coma and starts communicating. Personalities can change. Memories can be totally wiped out.

We didn't know if he would even be cognizant of what was going on. Since a state trooper could walk in and start asking him questions, it became even more crucial that someone was with him at all times.

The impact of the crash was so powerful that it blew out both of Caleb's eardrums while breaking all the bones in his ears and nearly all the bones in his face. Over the course of the next several weeks, we discovered that he had three broken ribs, a broken radius bone requiring surgery and medical plates and pins to set, a broken pelvis in three areas which also required surgical pinning, a shattered femur in his left leg requiring a titanium rod being surgically placed, along with cuts, bruising, abrasions, and road rash. All of this and he was wearing his seat belt.

He was so swollen that we didn't even know he had broken his right arm for over a week. We didn't know he developed a deep vein thrombosis for almost two weeks due to the intensity of his other injuries.

He also fractured the C7 vertebrae in his neck. While we were in the ICU trauma unit, we learned that they have a saying in the medical field: "C7? See you in heaven," because over 95 percent of people who break their C7 die when the vertebrae slices through or compresses the bundle of nerves that the C7 guards. We were told that the C7 nerve bundle is what tells your brain and body to breathe.

Thankfully, Caleb's fractured C7 didn't sever the bundle of nerves, but it did fling a piece of vertebrae into his jugular vein, slicing that open on the inside.

Most of these injuries were visible, but Caleb will attest that there are also internal, unseen scars that he will have for the rest of his life.

It's easy to see physical scars and wounds. You can see if they are old or new, or whether the wounds need to be stitched by a doctor or if a Band-Aid would be enough. These are the easy ones. But emotional wounds and scars are not as easy to detect—past abuses, hurts, guilt.

Emotional pain hurts so we protect it, covering it up while we try to live like those vulnerable areas aren't there. We're injured, so we use anger as a force field around us. Nobody bothers us and everybody stays away. "Don't talk to them. They're angry."

Or we deal with pain by an addiction—food, prescription drugs, work. How do we deal with the emotional pain without running to those pain-relieving addictions? In the days ahead, all three of us would have to answer that question for ourselves.

Myron preached a sermon about those hidden scars the year after the accident and said, "If you knew anything about me before the accident, you know that I did not put much stock in emotions. I did not put much stock in emotional scars or emotional wounds. I was a person who'd say, 'Ah, later for all that emotional stuff.' But I found out that emotional wounds and scars are very real. One thing I learned from this experience was not to say things like, 'I understand what you're going through.' I don't know how many times I heard, 'I know what you're going through.' We don't know because every single person handles things differently. We've learned that each of us deals with wounds differently.

"God made the human body amazingly resilient. For example, when you get a cut, your body immediately goes to work to heal it. You don't have to think about it or coordinate it—it just happens. Often, once the body has finished its work and the wound has closed, there is a scar. The scar is evidence of closure—no more blood, no more scabs, just skin.

"However, when we experience an emotional wound, our body does not naturally go into recovery mode. The old saying 'time heals all wounds' is not always true. We have to take an active role in processing what happened and asking the Lord for healing. When we give it to the Lord, he begins to work in our hearts. He eases the pain and grants us the ability to forgive the one who hurt us.

"There's also what I call 'invisible scars,' because they are the ones that we rarely ever talk about, yet they are as real as physical and emotional scars. These are the wounds that are caused inside the body of Christ. Misunderstandings, abandonments, or pouring our lives into people to see them walk away and talk badly about us later on.

"Did you know that the tongue has a certain type of tissue that does not scar when it is torn? I don't care how many times you may bite your tongue and hurt yourself, God has fixed it so that the tongue can virtually repair itself, and when it does, it leaves no scar.

"However, the only scar that the tongue could leave is when you use your tongue to speak against other people—it doesn't leave a physical scar, but it still leaves a scar.

"Sometimes wounds won't heal and scar over either. Sometimes it's because of antibiotic-resistant bacteria. When these bacteria get in, it presents a strong resistance to standard antibiotics. Wounds infected with this may have a bluish or greenish tinge to them due to bacteria consuming fluids in the wound and then releasing waste.

"Know anybody like this? They have wounds that they just won't allow to heal. It doesn't get better with time, it only gets worse—this constantly oozing wound. They are bound in depression, bitterness, and hatred. It consumes their life. In the physical, this turns into gangrene and the patient will lose a limb, or worse, they lose their life.

"Are you allowing your hurts to turn into hates? If so, ask yourself: Is it working? Has your hatred done you any good? Has your resentment brought you any relief, any peace? Has it granted you any joy?

"Let's say you get even. Let's say you get him back. Let's say she gets what she deserves. Let's say your fantasy of fury runs its ferocious course and you return all your pain with interest. Imagine yourself standing over the corpse of the one you have hated. Will you now be free?

"A few years after the boys' accident, I was talking with a pastor who also lost a son in a tragic accident. He told me there are only two directions you can choose in recovery: Either move forward or live in the past.

"Can I tell you, all those that are carrying around emotional and spiritual scars, God has a plan for your healing?

"He says in Isaiah 61:1–7 (MSG):

> The Spirit of God, the Master, is on me because God anointed me. He sent me to preach good news to the poor, heal the heartbroken, announce freedom to all captives, pardon all prisoners. God sent me to announce the year of his grace—a celebration of God's destruction of our enemies—and to comfort all who mourn, to care for the needs of all who mourn in Zion, give them bouquets of roses instead of ashes, Messages of joy instead of news of doom, a praising heart instead of a languid spirit. Rename them "Oaks of Righteousness" planted by God to display his glory. They'll rebuild the old ruins, raise a new city out of the wreckage. They'll start over on the ruined cities, take the rubble left behind and make it new. You'll hire outsiders to herd your flocks and foreigners to work your fields, but you'll have the title "Priests of God," honored as ministers of our God. You'll feast on the bounty of nations; you'll bask in their glory. Because you got a double dose of trouble and more than your share of contempt, your inheritance in the land will be doubled and your joy go on forever.

"Let our wounds and scars draw us to Christ. He will always meet us in our darkest hour. If we have emotional scars because of our wrong or unwise choices, we are reminded of the grace of his forgiveness and never-ending love. The truth is, God sometimes allows us to experience difficult situations—even scarring experiences—to sanctify us and draw us closer to him.

"Once the Lord has helped you work through your pain and wounds, your life will be a compelling testimony to the power of the Holy Spirit. God let our family's hearts be broken so that I could share with you that you are more than what has happened to you. Sometimes life can hurt. But that doesn't define who I am. God has bigger plans.

"Your scars do not define who you are."

Dad

Thought it'd be okay to give you a Father's Day card that was a little messed up. Because if anyone can fix it, you can!

When I saw this card, I knew that it was the right one. You are always the one that we can bring our "broken" areas to and you always do everything in your power to help. Thank you for being this family's rock and leader through this difficult time. There will be a great reward one day and I truly believe that Jacob is proud of you up there in Heaven. I love you, Dad.

Love,
Caleb
Father's Day
2016

ONE LESS WHY

EVEN IN THE WOMB, I could tell Caleb and Jacob were going to be completely different. Caleb seemed to be trying out for the Olympic gymnastics team as he rebounded off my rib cage. Jacob moved just enough to say, "Hey, I'm here, Mom."

With Caleb, I had morning sickness every day for months. I never got sick once with Jacob.

The same continued all of their childhoods. Same parents, but two polar-opposite kids in so many ways.

One strong-willed. One compliant.

One organized. One messy.

One a fighter. One a peacemaker.

One a writer. One an artist.

One time they joined efforts to "self-publish" a book. Caleb wrote *From Broken to Beautiful* and Jacob drew the illustrations. We gave copies to family, friends, and teachers for Christmas that year.

They were both always using those talents to bless me too. Caleb often writes very meaningful words to me in Mother's Day cards, for my birthday, that kind of thing.

Jacob knew my love for flowers and often drew them for me, painted them for me, and even hand-tooled them into leather for me. He definitely inherited his artistic bent from Myron's dad, Don.

Don and Elaine, "Granddad and Grammy," owned a saddle and tack store in Idaho and Don made gorgeous, custom saddle and leather works. We cherish the pieces that Don made for us before he passed away, just like we cherish the pieces Jacob created and left behind—precious heirlooms, more valuable than gold.

Just a few months before the accident, Jacob made me a home-made card. It's several pieces of printer paper stapled together, and it has several hand-drawn, beautiful flowers inside. Jacob compared me to beautiful, colorful, sweet flowers, and then he wrote:

> Seriously, though Mom, you are the most wonderful mother anyone could ever ask for. Thank you for all your love, help, and example-ship. Thank you for always being there, open, and receptive, and helpful when I need to talk. I hope that one day I have a wife that loves me and is there for me like you are. I appreciate everything that you do.
> Happy Mother's Day!
> Jacob Leavitt
> 5/10/15

What was painful to read right after the accident is now a cherished treasure.

Memories flitter through my mind of all of the walks that Jacob and I took together when I'd hear his heart—praying for his family, his classmates, his teachers, his church family, especially the teen ministry. Talking to God like the Father that he is.

Then memories flitter through of all of those talks we had on the long car rides. Times when I just wanted to put music on and zone out, but then I'd remember Myron and I counseling other parents to do their best to be "intentional" in their parenting, making use of any opportunity with your kids. Even if it's just spending time together, building a relationship. "One day, you'll be grateful," we'd tell them.

And I'd turn the radio down and we'd talk.

Our family has always been pretty upbeat, and we love to have fun, so naturally, some of my favorite memories involve sarcasm or a good laugh—or both.

One time, the boys and I were at a theme park using the annual passes we'd bought for the family for Christmas the year before. As the boys got older, that was a great way to keep from accumulating more Christmas "stuff" while also ensuring we'd spend time together the following year. Myron wasn't able to go with us that time, so it was just us three. It was almost Halloween, so the park transformed their nature boardwalk into a creepy, haunted trail.

Now let me tell you, I do *not* like to be scared, but the boys wanted to go, and hey, I was a thirty-something-year-old mom. I got this, right?

What happened? This thirty-something scaredy-cat mom became the front man for a whole group of young people scared out of their minds. Teenage boys tall enough to tower over me were huddled *behind* me as we were being chased by chainsaw-wielding fiends through the dry swamp bed. We would just catch our breath, when—*VROOM*—here comes another chainsaw.

Finally, *finally*. We could see the end of the boardwalk. As another chainsaw chaser advanced on us, we rounded a bend and . . . there. Maybe fifty yards away, near the end of this cursed path.

But, oh no. Not so easy. Out of nowhere, seriously, it's like he dropped from the trees. Another chainsaw freak descended and split our group in two. In the chaos, Caleb was separated from us and was stuck near the back half of the group. We were all stock-still for a second, eyeing the chainsaw, hearing only the rush of our heartbeat and the *VROOM*.

Keep in mind, now, that from the womb, Jacob was content with as little movement as possible. Totally laid back, never in a hurry. We often called him slowpoke while he embodied the "What's the rush? Life is beautiful." mantra.

On top of that, Jacob was always a stocky kid, so picture it: This short, stocky kid, maybe eight years old, was scared out of his wits at the front of the pack and I was right behind him. Caleb was at the very back, looking at us.

In a split second, Jacob's little legs lit out flying down the path just as fast as his feet would take him. He didn't stop until he was well past the end of the trail, clearing the boardwalk's exit and rounding the corner—not taking any chances.

I looked back at Caleb as if to say, "Sorry bud, you're on your own here," and took off too. The chainsaw guy looked at both of us and shrugged, like "Oh well," before turning to the rest of the group and terrorizing them.

Sides heaving, I finally caught up to Jacob. (Yes, Caleb followed soon after.) As the adrenaline rush faded, Caleb gave us a lashing for leaving him high and dry. That didn't last long because we all dissolved into laughter over the whole situation. Even Caleb had seen Jacob flee from that madman like a possessed kid. We had never seen him move that fast before.

It makes us smile even now. It struck me after the funeral that, "Hey—Jacob, the family slowpoke, *beat us there*. He's in heaven before us and will be there to greet us. How funny is that? The one who was always last actually got to heaven first."

These priceless memories also revealed part of God's answer to one of my questions: Why would you heal me from cancer and then take our son seventeen years later?

I still remember when his answer settled over me with complete soundness that brooked no further questioning: he healed me from cancer to allow me the opportunity to be a part of raising the boys with Myron—to help mold them, imparting truth, love, and character in them.

Raising my boys has been the greatest honor of my life—a GodPrint that perhaps pressed a little deeper in my heart than all the others.

Today, Lord, one thing that can keep me going is that I am one day closer to seeing Jacob. One more day is behind me, and I am one day closer to eternity where Jacob is.

Thank you for coming alongside me, not only allowing my questions but providing answers . . . and peace, even when no answer is seen—at least not yet. Thank you for being the solid rock I can stand on—in uncertainty, in the storms, when the waves are crashing all around me.

You are there. You lift me up and sustain me.

-From Jenny's private journal

23

BEST LAID PLANS

EVEN AT A YOUNG AGE, I have always been a meticulous planner. I had my whole life planned out before I even met Myron. I planned on graduating from college and getting married—to someone—on Valentine's Day of 2000. I would turn twenty-five that year and have graduated from college.

Wow, how different my life has turned out from all those self-made plans.

It took me years to really appreciate the fact that God had brought me a loyal, strong, dependable man who didn't cower away from adversity, but rose to the challenge. Despite everything that life would throw at us, he tries to tackle it with faith, tenacity, and yes, even humor.

People often ask me, tongue-in-cheek, "Jenny, how do you put up with him?"

I tell them, "He adds spice to my life. Without him, my life would be so boring."

Don't get me wrong, he also has lingering issues from life's experiences. Things he experienced in childhood and wounds that have been inflicted upon him by others, including me.

But I'm so grateful that I married a fighter. I wish it hadn't taken me so long to realize how much I needed that in a husband.

All our memories tied together as we stood in the ICU waiting room with Myron's mom and sister. As soon as they heard about the accident, they hopped on the next plane.

In the little waiting room, Myron came up alongside me and wrapped his arm around my shoulders, tucking me close. We'd been up for almost two days straight by then, and I was so exhausted that I just leaned there, trying to soak up some of his strength.

He gently held me close and said, "I need you to take my beautiful bride home so she can try to get some rest."

I felt so loved and cherished at that moment. Even during the swirling grief and uncertainty, my husband was thinking of my needs.

We gathered up our few things from the waiting room and headed down to the truck. My thoughts were getting the best of me as they drove me home. I looked down and saw Jacob's fluorescent orange USB cord and the tears started flowing all over again. I tried to rein them in, but the thoughts were quickly becoming a whirlwind of anxiety. Really, more like a living nightmare.

I'll never see Jacob again.

Oh God, please don't take Caleb while I'm gone.

How can I possibly go on with life?

How can people all around me be going on with life like everything is okay and our hearts weren't just shattered to pieces?

From my struggles against cancer and its aftereffects all these years, I had a few tools in the reservoir to help me combat the fear and corral those quickly spiraling feelings of despair. I just had a gut feeling that if I let myself ruminate on them, I would sink so low that I wasn't confident I'd be able to rise again. At that point, one of the things that kept me pressing forward was the thought that Caleb needed me.

I've always loved music and I knew that one of the things that really helped me a lot during those trying times of cancer was worshipping God through song. Either singing or just letting the words sink deep into my soul as I listened to it.

I told Myron's mom and sister about an album I had been listening to lately and that I needed to hear one of the songs. They were so gracious and kind to me. I know they'd never heard of Jeremy Camp, but they listened attentively as we drove the forty minutes home and "Be Still" played on the sound system.

The lyrics reminded me of Psalms 46:10, which became another lifeline of sorts for me in the days to come. When anxiety ripped through me and wanted dominion in my mind, I could make a choice to be still, knowing that my God is faithful and hears me, saving each tear I cry. Reminding me that he's able to hold me up, standing with me when I can't stand on my own strength. He's enough. That even when my heart is racing and fear threatens to take me out, his love endures forever. Even there, in those desolate places.

As the sweet, soulful song ends with a reassuring melody on the violin, it flows right into "Perfect Love," a song that brought me even more comfort.

Oh, God, my heart cried out. Yes. Here I am, Lord, drawing near. I'm crying out. Hear me, Lord. I need you. More than breath. More than life. I'm hanging on—even in the pain.

When the two songs ended, I stopped the album and told my family, "Thank you so much for letting me play them. I needed that."

Their cheeks were wet, too, as we rode on in silence. Then my mother-in-law spoke up from the back seat and said, "I can see why. Those songs are amazing."

Inside the house a little later, I was amazed to see that our church family had come and cleaned our home top to bottom, and had even brought fresh linens and pillows for my in-laws. After getting them situated, the weight of the last forty-eight hours settled over me.

Sleep. I desperately wanted to sleep. *Rest.*

Unfortunately, that would be harder to come by than I could have ever imagined.

Like a drowning man desperate for something stable, it felt like I was drowning in grief. My emotions pummeling me like waves.

Wave after wave of grief and uncertainty crashing over me . . . again, and again, and again.

Floundering in the water, my faith felt so small. I started to slip under, feeling like all hope was lost.

Trying to pray, but the words were muddled. Incoherent. Flitting from one thought to the next.

But then, I came to the rock that is higher than I. Jesus stretched out his hand, helping me when I didn't even have the strength to form a word, let alone cry out.

With his help, I climbed up on the rock, thanking God for the stability and the anchor that it provides-immovable, unshakable, and able to weather the storm I'm in.

I felt the rock giving me the strength to rise above the storm and above the waves. It's only when I keep my feet firmly planted in the center of the rock that I feel this strength, this renewed strength, flowing within me.

Every time that my foot slips or I fall back in the water, I know that if I can just get back to that rock, he will anchor me again.

~From Jenny's private journal

BAD DREAMS

I'M SURE MY EYES MUST have looked wild with fear as I called out, "Myron, I need you!"

I had been reading Philippians 4 to Caleb when suddenly, he began thrashing violently and uttering completely unintelligible words—guttural sounds full of intense emotion and pain.

We still weren't sure how much of "our" Caleb was left after the TBI.

Would he remember us? Would he have brain damage? Would he retain his personality? Or would he be completely different?

We'd already lost Jacob. Would Caleb never be the same too?

As I watched him swing his arms to strike a nurse, I thought, Oh, God. Is this it? Is Caleb here in body but gone from us forever? Did you spare him only to allow him to never be the same? Oh, God. NO. Please, no.

I watched in horror as our beloved son looked straight into the doctor's eyes and hissed out menacing words which rapidly turned into outright screams.

"I know what you're trying to do, and it won't work. You're not going to get me. No, you won't take me."

I was gently, but firmly, pushed out to the hallway while medical personnel charged into the room. Fleeing to the waiting room, my only thought was that I *needed* Myron. I needed his strength and wisdom.

He caught my eye looking through the little window and jumped up to meet me.

"What is it? What happened? Is something wrong?"

"It's Caleb!"

"What happened?" he asked as we ran down the hallway. I was so panicked I could hardly think straight, let alone speak coherently.

"I don't know. It's like he's going crazy."

On top of everything else, Caleb had contracted MRSA, so we had to gown up and use precautions every time we entered the room. After several more painstaking moments, Myron stepped up to Caleb's side as he continued to lash out verbally and physically, leaned over him and looked him right in the eyes.

Out in the hallway, I watched as Caleb said, "Dad! Dad! They're coming after us, Dad. Don't let them get us."

Myron tried to speak calmly and reassure Caleb with, "Son, it's okay."

But Caleb would just cry out again, "No, Dad, it's not okay! They're trying to get me, Dad. Don't let them."

We had no idea what he was seeing in his mind or living out in the semi-coherent dream state he was in.

The medical team had to strap him down because he was fighting them and screaming, "No, you're not gonna take me!"

As Myron tried to calm Caleb's fears, assuring him that he was safe, nurses administered sedatives. Caleb continued to exclaim, "I know what they're doing. They want us. They're going to kill us. Dad, you've got to stop them. You've got to stop them."

After what seemed like an eternity and a lot of prayer, the meds kicked in and he slowly relaxed and drifted off to sleep. Myron came out in the hallway and wrapped me in a hug as the emotional roller coaster we'd been riding on slowly came to a stop.

ICU psychosis, the ICU staff informed us. Quite common in extreme trauma cases. Patients experience severe anxiety, hear voices, hallucinate, become agitated and paranoid, and even violent like Caleb had. Especially when head trauma meets a patient's first exposure to narcotic pain meds.

Gosh, I thought, just what kind of nightmare was he having? Was this a spiritual assault? Was he reliving the accident? Was it from the medications? Or was it all intertwined?

Caleb never experienced another episode of ICU psychosis again, but the nightmares plagued him almost every time he went to sleep until one day he told the doctors, "That's it. Take me off all the narcotic pain meds. Stop them."

The doctors told him, "You can't just stop them."

Caleb was twenty years old, and now fully cognizant as he said, "Stop the meds. No more. I can't do those nightmares anymore. These narcotics are spiritual."

They put him on a regimen of Tylenol—ibuprofen—Tylenol—ibuprofen, with Benadryl at night to help him sleep. He never had narcotics again, even with all the pain he was going through.

The nightmares stopped.

Sometime later, Caleb and I talked about that time in the trauma ICU unit and those nightmares. He said: "I remember the pain. I remember one night I literally could not sleep the whole night because there was an intense pain under my ribs. And the nurse said, 'Why don't you go back on the pain meds?'

"And I said, 'No, I'll just ride out the pain. It's not worth it to me to go back on them.'"

I asked Caleb, "Because the nightmares were that bad?"

"Well, that's the thing. It was like the same nightmare over and over, and it didn't feel like a nightmare. It felt like it was real. I still remember the time that made me say, 'I'm done with these.'

"I remember driving down a curving road through the woods to a house made completely of glass. At the beginning of the dream, there was a group of us and we were going inside. I knew it was a secret meeting, but I don't remember what it was for. I don't remember faces or anything, just that there were people in the car and in the house too.

"All the lights went out, and then we were all running through the woods, and I was catching glimpses of things behind me. I turned and looked, and it was like a dragon, but more like a de-mon-dragon. It was chasing after me. I remember thinking in my dream, 'If it catches me, I'm going to die. And if I die right now, I'm going to hell. I'm fighting for my life right now.'

"I kept running through the woods and I got to a clearing where there was a mountain edge. I ran up to it and stopped. I turned around and I saw this thing come out of the woods. It stopped and was looking right at me. When it came out of the woods, it was just me and it on the edge of the mountain. I had nowhere else to go.

"I remember there was this fear that I felt whenever I saw this thing. I can still see it in my mind. It was just like . . . *darkness*.

"I thought, There is nothing I can do to get away from this now. I can't run anymore. To this day, I can still feel that. It was that deep.

"That's when I woke up and said, 'Whatever these drugs are, they need to stop.' After that, the nightmares stopped too."

While I was deeply thankful that Caleb had escaped the night-mares of his sleep, we were still very much in the middle of a wak-ing nightmare of our own. If Caleb's were drug-induced, then what kind of nightmare were *we* in? Because surely this was just a bad dream. We'd wake up and all would be well.

But it wasn't a nightmare. There would be no waking up to find out it was all a bad dream. This was our life now.

And this time, there was no running down a boardwalk to flee the madman.

It's almost automatic to look for an exit in struggle,
but it is often God's will to go through it . . .
No experience in life is wasted if you learn from it. . . .
If hell can cut off your relationships,
you will never survive a storm.
—Jacob Leavitt's notes from Pastor Joe Campbell's
sermon "Surviving Struggles" (5/13/15)

HOMESICK

WHILE CALEB WAS STILL IN the trauma ICU, Myron had to positively identify Jacob's body. Then we had to prepare to bury our youngest son. If you had told me a week prior that I would be in a funeral home, sitting at the table with Myron and the director while we decided on a casket and order of service for Jacob, I would never have believed it was possible. Those tragedies happen to *other* people. Not us.

Yet, there we were. Then came all the other difficult tasks associated with losing a loved one.

Questions like, who would write the obituary? I wished Caleb were awake—he's such a good writer that I think he would have done a great job. He wasn't awake, though, so I took on the task. What mother ever thinks she'll write her own child's obituary?

Then we also had to decide what clothes we should pick out for Jacob to be buried in. Again, I wished Caleb were able to give us feedback for this. We finally decided on Jacob's favorite church clothes along with slides for shoes instead of his fancier dress shoes. That boy loved his slides. Oh, and we couldn't forget his favorite-colored socks. He had so many pairs and loved to coordinate them with his outfits. We had to go through the messy room to find everything and then we took it to be dry-cleaned before we dropped it off at the funeral home.

On top of notifying out-of-town family and friends, we also had to prepare the funeral notice for the paper, the program for the service, the items we wanted on the memorial service tables, and the list went on and on. The stress on our bodies was so much that Myron and I both started losing our hair. We learned later that traumatic stress can do that to you. Honestly though, at that point neither one of us really cared. Our hair was the last thing on our minds.

We chose to do two separate funeral and memorial events in the hopes that Caleb would be awake and able to attend at least one of them. The first Saturday after the accident, we had a small graveside service for Jacob. Since Caleb was still in a coma, we made the choice to video everything so he could watch it later if he wanted to. The following Saturday we had a much bigger memorial service at the church.

I don't know what we would have done or how we would've made it through all of that, while also being there for Caleb and his multiple surgeries, without our church family. They provided food, housework, laundry, rides for out-of-town family that flew in, along with preparing everything for the services, with our input and approval. It is the understatement of the century to say that they were a blessing to our family.

Caleb began to slowly come back to us just the day before the memorial service on September 12, 2015. Myron was there in the middle of the night as Caleb finally became alert enough to ask, "Where is Jacob, Dad?"

Myron had to tell him about the wreck and then break the news to him that his younger brother passed away. I'm glad it was

Myron, so steady and strong, who was there for this moment and not me.

But there were still more questions.

What are you supposed to wear for your child's funeral? Who would've ever thought, *Hm, that's something I'll need to decide someday?*

Yet, there I was, standing in the closet, trying to figure out what to wear to our seventeen-year-old son's burial service. How on earth was I going to make it through this day?

We'd already had several talks with our pastor and the church was rallying behind us in prayer. Sometimes, like that day, we could feel those prayers give us strength to face the hours to come.

In one of those conversations, our pastor shared with us the new insight he had received from God's Word and wanted to focus on at the funeral, with our permission.

He said that God had been reminding him of the Scripture that tells us that we have great treasure inside of us as Christ's followers. The verses (2 Corinthians 4:7–9) liken us to jars of clay in this world, something that is easily broken, yet holds precious treasure. Pastor Meyer told us that he saw Jacob as one of those clay vessels that, upon breaking, would release that precious treasure to be poured out into the world.

Shortly after that conversation, I was going through some of Jacob's old church notebooks and found this note that he'd written back in 2013 during Pastor Tony Chase's sermon on "Earthen Vessels": *The treasure is deposited within us when we bow our knee to Jesus.*

It was a poignant confirmation in a much-needed hour.

After another long walk the morning of the funeral, trying desperately to pray, God, in his gracious mercy dropped a precious nugget of truth in my soul that settled inside like an anchor. A small whisper across my soul that changed the whole trajectory of my day.

If I'm going to be brutally honest, sometimes it feels like I'm not cut out for the work that it takes to break through these trials here on this earth. It would be so much easier for this life to be over and for our eternal life to start. I have confidence that God's Word is true, I'm forgiven, and the heaven that awaits believers is beyond our wildest imagination. I yearn for it.

Don't get me wrong—it's not like I have a death wish or anything. I'm very grateful that even in the depths of despair, I never experienced suicidal thoughts.

The Apostle Paul (in Ephesians) said that the *easiest* path would be for him to die and be with Christ. Then he reminds us that the real, true sacrifice would be to continue to live so that others can hear the good news and make heaven their home. For me, Jenny Leavitt, the true sacrifice will not be in leaving this life. The true sacrifice will be getting up each day, submitting to God, living for him, and sharing his love with others.

Until the day that Jesus decides is my day to go home.

Maybe you've felt this way too. Maybe you've struggled to feel at ease in a world filled with so much pain and darkness and have longed for the relief of heaven. You are not alone. But I would challenge you in the same way I've had to challenge myself. What would the *real* sacrifice mean for you? Giving up? Or fighting?

For me, when I get in this pattern of thinking of going home to Jesus, I have to pause and reflect on those undeniable GodPrint moments—those times he's intervened so intentionally that I can *feel* his hand clutching me. My work is not in heaven. My work is here on earth—no matter how difficult that calling feels some days. The same is true for you.

But the day we buried our seventeen-year-old son, I wasn't quite so strong. I just wanted to be with Jacob, in the presence of our Father.

As I walked and prayed early that morning, I tried to work through all these conflicting, unstable feelings. I asked for him to speak to me and, faithful as always, he did.

In a flash of understanding, like a siren call to my heart, he reminded me of Jesus's encouragement to ask God for "daily bread." Jesus also told us that *he* is that bread.

I knew, *just knew*, that God was reminding me that no matter what happens, he will be everything I needed to get through that horrible day. He would sustain me.

Today. One day at a time. One hour a time. One minute at a time, if necessary.

Today, he would never leave me.

Today, he would provide for us.

Today, he would give us all we needed to get through this.

Tomorrow? He would be all I needed for then too.

Myron stepped into the room, concern written all over his face as he looked at me. He was trying to see how I was doing, but I could see his agony too. We had to do this. We had to drive to the cemetery and bury our son.

As Myron wrapped his arms around me, I chose to speak life. To remind myself, "We have a good Father, and his heart is good."

Earlier in that same notebook of church notes, I found this entry Jacob made from Pastor Jeremy Meyer's sermon, "The Works of the Lord are Great," from 2012:

His promise:

1. Resurrection of the dead
2. Eternal life
3. Heaven
4. Wipe away every tear
5. No more pain

Those promises from Scripture were bread for me at that moment. They sustained me when nothing else could.

That September Saturday that we buried Jacob, sweat rolled down my face even though it was morning, because summer in

Florida is sweltering. I liken it to living in a sauna. A Christian comedian likened it to walking on the surface of the sun.

As Myron and I leaned into each other staring at Jacob's silver casket just feet in front of us, I thought of all these things. I thought about the broken vessel inside that box, and I whispered to Myron as the tears flowed, "He's not there. That's just the shell. He's not there."

One day, the ground will crack open and the dead in Christ will rise first.

That means Jacob will beat us home.

One day, we who are alive and remain will join him in eternal life.

One day, all of Jesus's people will be rewarded with heaven.

One day, Jesus will intimately wipe every tear from our eyes.

One day, all my pain will be gone. No more cancer scares. No more back pain for Myron. No more soul pain for either of us.

On a daily basis, you either enhance or
diminish your relationship with the Father,
through your daily habits.
—Jacob (handwritten note in his Bible)

RETURN OF SARCASM

CALEB WAS SLOWLY REGAINING HIS personality, hints of sarcasm and all. Thank God, he was going to be all right. Our son was still there. Not an angry, distorted version, but the Caleb that we've always known.

Sometimes, when I would be out in the waiting room visiting with the folks that came to sit vigil with us, we would reminisce and laugh about good times. But I can tell you that the laughter bubbling up inside of me as I watched Caleb joke with his nurses was like a balm for my aching heart.

Just like when I faced the possibility of my own death from cancer years ago and survived, Caleb had also faced death and survived. Just like me, he could go forward in this life, but never go back. That line of thinking generated all kinds of questions in my mind.

Remember when I said that the most humbling and startling revelation for me after going through cancer was when I considered what might have happened if I'd rebelled against God's will for my life and done my own thing, choosing college over him? And how I've often wondered if that one decision made the difference in whether I survived the cancer?

Well, one day in the fall of 2015, those what-if questions spurred new ones.

What if . . . Jacob had ridden home with me?

What if . . . the boys had left earlier?

What if . . . there was something we could have, or should have, done differently?

As I took the trash out one day, something Pastor Campbell said long ago ricocheted through my brain: "There's no manure in an empty pen."

You see, taking the trash out was just one more chore that remained undone now that Jacob was gone and Caleb was incapacitated. Guilt overwhelmed me again as I remembered all those times that I'd harped on the boys about not taking care of their responsibilities. What I wouldn't give at that moment to have the time back again. I'd take overflowing trash (the "manure") with my boys alive and healthy over this empty, hollow house (the "pen") any day.

Tragedy sure has a way of revealing what we take for granted in this life. *Who* we take for granted.

I thought of all the memories we would never be able to make now. We'd never see him graduate or get married or give us grandkids. He would never have an eighteenth birthday celebration.

I thought about how much I missed his jovial personality. I missed telling him, "I love you, Jacob." I sorrowed that I didn't get a final goodbye. I mourned over my many parenting regrets.

I can look back before the accident and see how God tried to shore up the weak areas in my life and even in our family because he knew what was coming. I can't blame it on him because there were still weak areas of my life that I had not addressed. Character issues that I had failed to address became blatantly obvious after the accident. I can't ascribe that to God. That's on me.

But even then, I could also see how the lessons that we learned going through life's trials served to prepare us in many ways for the tragedy that we were going through now.

I learned that God is my strength and that I couldn't make it without him. I learned that even when I doubt, he is there to help me, but I must do my part and ask for his help.

I learned that we have a real, very real, enemy who hates us. If he can't kill us, he will do everything he can to derail us, push us into despair or fear, or whisper lies to us that sound so believable that it's hard to distinguish them from the truth.

I learned that we have a God who gives us everything that we need for the battle and expects us to do our part in the fight. He doesn't leave us alone, but fights for us and with us, as well.

I learned that he gave me a husband whose strength, faith, leadership, and loyalty could be trusted.

I learned that the King is very aware of the details of my life, including my sorrow. I could find rest for my soul in him.

I learned that God met every financial need that we had. We never lacked the necessities of life.

We saw firsthand how God uses his people to help his sons and daughters.

These same lessons held true after the accident. GodPrint after GodPrint after GodPrint.

The constants that bound them all together? Jesus and his people.

Myron told a group one time when he was sharing our story, "When the wreck happened and we lost our son and our oldest son was in the hospital for months, our faith was strong enough to handle that because of what we'd already been through. We could have complained all the way through it. We could have complained about the cancer. We could have complained about the back injury. We could have complained about losing everything and being homeless. We could have complained about all the different aspects of our lives. What good would that do?

"In reality, God was preparing us for what was coming on down the road. We have no idea what's coming, but he does.

"We'd already made up our minds: Whatever happens in my life, I'm going to be faithful to you." Myron continued, "God says, 'The devil is subject to me and can only go as far as I say.' None of this catches God by surprise. The key when you're going through it is to know that he's there with you."

Myron and I had some honest discussions about how hard this battle with grief was. The mental battles alone were horrendous for me, let alone the emotional roller coaster. Overjoyed at Caleb's progress on a good day just to have a setback that same night. Gratitude for a sweet memory of Jacob just to plummet into the depths of pain driving through the car wash we went to together the week before the wreck. I never imagined that memories of washing a car with the boys would bring me such pain.

Myron reminded me what I already knew to be true—but had lost sight of. He reminded me that as God's sons and daughters, we have everything we need in Christ. He reminded me that we can often see Satan's tactics at work if we stop and look, just as we can see God's handiwork in our lives if we stop and look. Satan wants our mind to be his playground, but God has given us the power to take control of our minds when we let God cleanse and renew it each day. Each of us face the same choice daily and must decide who will rule our minds.

Emotions are great locators but terrible navigators—telling you where you are but not what to do. I know that I must make a conscious effort to retrain my thoughts toward God and gratitude when melancholy thoughts sweep through my soul.

But why it is so hard? Thoughts of fear, anxiety, and worry push out words of worship, faith, and peace in my mind, troubling even my sleep. Just when I think I've got one area under control, it feels like another fire pops up in my mind, seeking attention.

For some reason, my mind wandered back to that day all those years ago when little Jacob cut the pool and tried to tape it up to cover his guilt. Maybe it was because we'd been reminiscing about him and trying to figure out what to write for his obituary. Maybe I just needed to remember laughter.

Either way, at first the memory made me chuckle, but I quickly sobered as I realized that just like Jacob tried to shift his guilt and blame, it would be all too easy for me to forget that we are at war. How often do we fail to see how our choices also affect the outcome?

In warfare, people get wounded. People die. So the crucial question became: Who is our real enemy here? The enemy of our souls is ruthless. He will constantly assault our hearts just because of who we are—children of God, made in his image.

Satan is the real enemy, coming to steal, kill, and destroy, but Jesus said, "I have come that they may have life, and life more abundantly." That's his promise. So, he's not the one who caused the cancer, the back injury, or the accident that changed our family forever.

One time in Bible study, Myron asked, "What is the message that hell is putting into our minds that is leaving us terrorized? What is that message that plays repeatedly in our minds when we're trying to go to sleep? How are we going to pay that bill? How is this going to work out at my job? What's going to happen? Fear, fear, fear—trying to figure out how I can fix this problem or that problem.

"The good news is that once we can name that fear, the giant is defeated. Here's an old proverb for you: 'A devil exposed is a devil defeated.' Once we recognize that fear for what it is, we have the right to say, 'I know who you are and I know what you're doing.'"

When it seems like all hell has broken out against me, then I must choose to trust in his faithfulness, just as the author of Lamentations does in 3:21–23: "But this I call to mind, and therefore I have hope: the steadfast love of the LORD never ceases; his mercies never come to an end; they are new every morning; great is your faithfulness."

You must choose to trust in his faithfulness too. You must choose to claim the truth that somehow, God's steadfast love will make it all right in the end.

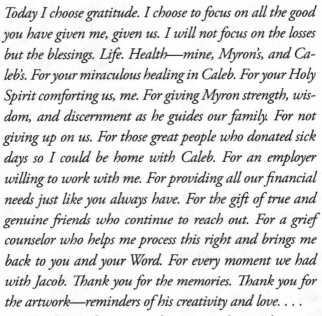

Today I choose gratitude. I choose to focus on all the good you have given me, given us. I will not focus on the losses but the blessings. Life. Health—mine, Myron's, and Caleb's. For your miraculous healing in Caleb. For your Holy Spirit comforting us, me. For giving Myron strength, wisdom, and discernment as he guides our family. For not giving up on us. For those great people who donated sick days so I could be home with Caleb. For an employer willing to work with me. For providing all our financial needs just like you always have. For the gift of true and genuine friends who continue to reach out. For a grief counselor who helps me process this right and brings me back to you and your Word. For every moment we had with Jacob. Thank you for the memories. Thank you for the artwork—reminders of his creativity and love. . . .

Thank you for surrounding me with your love, joy, and peace, and for not giving up on me throughout all of this. It's just the opposite. You have been faithful to walk this road with me—with us—and I am already seeing some of the "good" you're bringing from it. Thank you for helping me choose gratitude today. Help me to re-center daily. To abide daily.

I will be forever grateful for: My salvation, Jacob's salvation, Myron—a man seeking your face, Caleb—holding on to you even when it's hard, the friends you've brought us who are standing by us, and you, Jesus—you've never left me, never forsaken me.

~From Jenny's private journal

You Matter

CALEB CONTINUED TO SLOWLY RECOVER, even amid more surgeries and procedures. He was moved from the trauma ICU to the trauma step-down unit, and then to the inpatient rehab unit that he would call home for the next ten weeks.

There was an underlying tension over the possibility that Caleb could be charged for vehicular manslaughter in his brother's death. Back and forth our attorney and investigators went with law enforcement, insurance companies, and judicial proceedings.

Our investigator interviewed the sole witness and found inconsistencies that questioned the state's determination of Caleb's fault. Then we found out that the other driver had already been sentenced. We were never even informed that he had gone to court, and it didn't make the news. We were told that the judge essentially threw the book at him, but since it was his first DUI offense, and the state had ticketed Caleb, the prosecution's hands were tied.

According to public records, he was guilty of the charge of DUI with a blood alcohol level of .08 or greater. He pled nolo contendere (accepted the charge without admitting guilt) and received probation for one year, jail for one day, fifty hours of community service, DUI school, paid a fine, attended a victim impact panel, had his car immobilized for ten days, had his driver's license suspended for 180 days, and had to drive with an interlock device for six months.

Considering our overwhelming loss and trauma, it felt like a slap in the face.

Yet, even amid such turmoil and pain, Myron astounded me when we were at a meeting with the attorneys and investigator. Caleb was still in the rehab facility when we were brought in and interviewed. As the meeting was wrapping up, Myron said, "Is there any way I can talk to the families or to those two young men?"

The attorneys said, "Why do you want to do that?"

Myron assured them, "Look, it's not what you might think. If it had not been for Jesus, I could have been in their shoes because I was doing stupid stuff like that when I was their age. And if nothing else, I want them to know that I've forgiven them."

I sat there and thought, Wow. I forgive them, but I don't know if I could do that.

Eventually, he was able to meet both fathers of the other vehicle's occupants. One of them basically said, "Okay. Yeah, I'll pass the message along. Thanks."

The other one listened a little bit more, but basically said the same thing. At that point, Myron let it drop, telling me, "I did what I felt like God was telling me to do."

Looking back, he thinks that helped cement his decision to forgive and to be able to confidently say, "I forgive them."

I remember when it hit me that out of the four young men involved in the accident, it appeared that Jacob might have been the only one who was ready to meet his Creator—something I hadn't been completely sure of in my darkest moments following the accident.

One morning just before Jacob's memorial service, my heart was so heavy. I hadn't been sleeping well, and even though it was only around 6:00 a.m., I had already been for a long walk and straightened up the kitchen. Trying to be quiet because my mother- and sister-in-law were sleeping nearby, I went into Jacob's room and shut the door. I decided to see if I could find anything else for the church to use at his service.

I desperately prayed, "*God, I need to know* that Jacob wasn't playing church games with you. I need a peace that he's with you."

Tears drenching my shirt, I began to sort through the mess that was Jacob's room. He had a great, big, compassionate heart, but boy, was he messy. I used to shake my head in wonder when I would see him cleaning his white sneakers to a sparkly shine while his room was a disaster area.

I began moving folders, notebooks, paper scraps, art supplies. Good grief! How much stuff did Jacob shove in these drawers, anyway?

I stumbled on what looked like a two-page handwritten poem. Caleb was the writer and Jacob was the artist, so I didn't even give it a second thought. Something prompted me to look at the second page, though. There—at the very end of the poem—Jacob had signed and dated it.

February 2015.

Just six months before he died.

When he was growing up, Jacob repeatedly got in trouble for carving his name on desks, bed frames, dressers, or the dining room hutch. That boy loved his name. When I saw the signature, that's when I knew it was not a copied poem for school.

I turned as my in-laws came running into the room to see what was wrong. I didn't even realize that I had cried out, startling them. Grasping the papers to my chest, I exclaimed, "Look at this treasure that God gave to us. We have to take it to the hospital and show Myron."

I didn't know it, but back in February, around the same time I was privately recommitting our sons to the Lord, God was doing some behind-the-scenes work on Jacob's heart. Wrestling with him—not giving in until Jacob was changed, just as his biblical namesake had been. God was answering my prayer from years ago when we had that family discussion and I told Jacob I was praying he would have his own wrestling-with-God-until-breakthrough moment.

What a precious, priceless treasure. What an amazing God we serve that hears our heart's cries for our children and works when no one knows and no one sees. Such a faithful God. He prepared Jacob to meet him six months ahead of time.

We later verified with his teachers that this was not an assignment. No, I'm convinced this was all God's doing.

Holding Me
The road was dark and dreary,
My eyes were getting weary.
I could not see
My hand in front of me
But I felt your hand holding me.

The conditions grew so bleak,
That I could hardly hear you speak.
The winds blew like a monsoon
And I wondered if relief would come soon
But I felt your hand holding me.

While my eyes grew ever dim,
Fear boiled over the brim.
I cried out in shame
And turned to you with the blame
But I felt your hand holding me.

I wanted to turn back,
As my temperance began to crack
But in my heart I knew
I had crossed the Rubicon with you
But I felt your hand holding me.

You said that you had a plan,
But how could you use such a sinful man?
You said I was able
My mind said I was unstable
But I felt your hand holding me.

Your words brought me back alive,
Like a musical reprive.
My heart beat again
My mind no longer thought of sin
But still I felt your hand holding me.

The path did not get lax,
And left me no time to relax.
The Evil one tried to tear us asunder
Throughout the midst of the thunder
But still I felt your hand holding me.

The road's end was drawing near,
And my eyes began to tear.
I finally saw that Glorious City
And had no room for my unholy self-pity
But still I felt your hand holding me.

My heart skipped a beat
As I went dancing down the street.
I was finally in this wonderful place
That was full of your mercy and grace!
At last I saw you, face to marvelous face . . .

Your hand had held me the whole way.

Jacob Leavitt
February 2015

When I found "Holding Me" it solidified the thought that God took the time to make sure Jacob was ready while also granting the other three young men the opportunity to search their hearts before their own appointment with death.

Because each life is valuable to him. Every life matters.

Twenty-four hours before the accident, Jacob and I were taking home some friends after the dress rehearsal for the special event we had all been a part of. Jacob had been wanting to be involved for a long time, but his dad and I wanted him to be responsible in other areas before we would allow him to have an added responsibility.

We'd finally allowed him to join the light ministry team, and this was the first dress rehearsal that he'd ever participated in.

While I was driving them home, he said, "Mom, you just don't realize how much this is going to touch people's lives."

He told us how special the finale song was that the drama team used as a lip sync. "You guys have got to hear this song. Listen to the words."

As he played the song for us, he was sharing part of his heart as well. He believed God would use the song "Matter" by For King and Country, to show people how much they matter to him.

The next night, Jacob stepped into eternity. He got to leave behind all the things we waste our time on. All the vain attempts to try to make our lives matter.

After the accident, I remember telling Myron that I just wanted to know that Jacob's life mattered. Then I remembered the song Jacob had shared with us the night before. I remembered how excited he was to see God use it to draw people to his love.

As our church family rallied around us to help plan Jacob's memorial, we shared the idea of somehow using the song at the service. We didn't know how, but we just felt like it needed to be included. They came up with an idea that blew our minds. While the choir sang "Matter," teens and adults alike held up signs telling everyone there, "YOU MATTER."

Teachers. Classmates. Family members. Football team. Friends. Doctors (Yes, his doctors came to the service). Parents. Brother.

You matter.

To Jacob . . . and to God.

Several months later, Caleb decided to write the band to express our family's heartfelt thanks:

Dear For King and Country,

I don't know if you will ever get this, but I hope you guys do. I wanted to thank you for allowing God to lead your lives into what he has planned for you guys. Your last CD touched my family, especially through our recent hardship. Tragedy struck our family . . . We were at a church event late one night and we had just left after cleaning our church when we were involved in a fatal car accident. My brother passed away that night. This accident changed our family in such a large way, but we still have hope in knowing that Jacob was a Christian when he died.

The week before the accident, Jacob listened to your song "Matter" something like 17 times. We used it in our church play and he loved the message of hope that it portrayed for people. You guys had a great impact on his final days and I'm so grateful for that. Throughout my recovery, your music was also an encouragement to my life. Some days were so hard, but listening to your music and other songs like it, I was able to push through and get stronger. I was able to go and see you again at the 2016 Winter Jam and your music brought tears to my eyes. I could just see Jacob looking down and singing along with us at that moment.

Thank you again for being willing to continue to make music, even during difficult times. It really does make a difference and I don't think you'll truly know just how many people you've helped until you guys reach heaven. Never stop letting God use your lives to help others.

Thanks again.

He was surprised to receive a personal reply a short time later:

Caleb,

Thank you so much for sharing your story with us! We are humbled that the band's songs brought hope through such a difficult time. Jacob seemed to have been a wonderful guy, and we are sorry to hear of your family's loss. Thank you for reaching out. I sent this out to our whole team. We greatly appreciate your support and will be praying for continual peace for your family.

    fK&C Team

SAY YES

WHEN THEY MOVED CALEB TO the inpatient rehab facility to learn how to walk and function all over again, I wore a hoodie every day inside even though it was ninety-eight degrees outside. The little, hard sofa that also served as a bed for whoever stayed the night with him was directly below the AC vent. I was freezing as I stretched my legs out in front of me, reading quietly as Caleb napped after his morning sessions.

I remember the familiar sounds of the busy facility around us. Nurses and doctors coming in and out. Therapists coming to get us for the next grueling round of teaching Caleb how to function with a broken arm, broken leg, broken ribs, broken tail bone, and TBI. All while wearing a C-collar too.

It was way too easy to slip into the wells of grief in those quiet times of Caleb's naps, but with the sounds of footsteps in the hallway muted by the closed door, I remember thinking, *This isn't the time to dwell on the magnitude of the loss.*

Even as we mourned Jacob, there was hope we would see him again. Now was the time to focus on what God had given Caleb—a second chance at life.

Just like I couldn't stand pity when I was going through cancer, Caleb couldn't stand it either, so I tried my best to arrive every morning with a good attitude, encouraging him as we started the day's therapy together. I tried to be firm, but compassionate, while also trying not to baby him. Well, at least not too much.

Each day was full of several different therapy sessions—physical therapy, occupational therapy, cognitive therapy, and group therapy. After a short break for lunch and rest, the afternoon held even more sessions.

After one particularly grueling day, Caleb told me, "Mom, I know that you've been through cancer and that was probably the hardest thing you've ever been through. But this is the hardest thing I've ever been through."

I told him, "Oh, son. Not so. At least with the cancer, it was my body, my health, my own future at stake. But this? It's ripping my heart to shreds."

These were our children. One was gone and one was battling for his life. I knew that Caleb would battle survivor's guilt, although I didn't know that's what it was called at the time. I knew it would take all that stubbornness he possessed to see him through this recovery. My heart broke as I saw him struggle just to sit up in bed. My independent son was forced to depend on others for everything.

Yet, even with all of that, there was some laughter and good times in the rehab facility. We saw his face light up when they brought in the therapy dog for visits. On days when the pain wasn't quite so bad, I saw him joke around with the nursing staff or with the guys from church who came to spend time with him.

I still chuckle when I think about some of the word associations he came up with in the cognitive-therapy sessions.

One time, the therapist was trying to help him think of creative ways to remember some of the doctors' names. Finding words that rhyme was one of the strategies she told him about. I still remember the look on her face when Caleb spouted off the name of a well-known terrorist because the name rhymed with one of the doctor's. With a shocked and mortified look, but also with a good dose of humor, the therapist said, "Wow—how about we don't call the doctor a terrorist?"

We were amazed how God brought medical professionals into our lives that were competent, professional, and caring when Caleb needed it most. From the first responders on the scene of the accident, to the emergency room personnel, to the ICU staff, and on through his months at the rehab unit: GodPrints.

Many of them took a personal interest in Caleb and would even stop by when their shift was over or on their days off to see how he was doing. In much the same way that we saw God's hand leading me to Gainesville and the team of doctors there, we knew that God had provided these wonderful people for us now.

As a matter of fact, the therapists at the rehab facility had such an impact on Caleb that after he was up and walking well, we drove to the facility so that they could see that their work was not in vain. Caleb wanted to personally thank them and even apologize for the attitude that he gave them when they were trying to help him.

One of the few pictures that I have of that time is of him standing between two of his former therapists, smiles all around. We took Caleb's medical devices with us that day and donated them to the rehab facility like I'd donated my wigs, turbans, and scarves to the American Cancer Society.

Most people who meet Caleb today have no idea that he endured such horrific physical trauma. He barely has a limp when he walks, and his outgoing, outspoken personality is intact.

Sometime later, Caleb and I were talking about those days when I asked him, "Do you remember when you were in the rehab facility and there was a new doctor who filled in on the weekend and didn't know you? He looked at your file out in the hallway and when he walked in the room, he just stood there for a minute. He looked down at the file, and then looked back up at you. You were sitting up and talking to us and he said, "Wow. I was not expecting you to look as good as you do."

"That was the same doctor who said, 'When you are forty, you're going to feel like you're eighty.' And you told him, 'No, I'm not.'"

It wasn't all victories, though. When I looked in his eyes, I saw the agony there and I realized there was so much more going on in that mind. I knew how much talking to a counselor had helped me, so I encouraged him to meet with one as well.

There were times I felt like I was going to drown underneath this tsunami of tumultuous emotions. Wave after wave after wave of guilt, grief, sorrow, and fear would pound me relentlessly.

I knew if I felt that way, I could only imagine what Caleb was experiencing. He was always the responsible older brother and now his younger brother had died while he was driving. I knew he would think that somehow Jacob's death was his fault. Even though it wasn't.

I had to bring Caleb to the feet of Jesus repeatedly because some things are just too big for me to carry.

Often life gets complicated, feelings getting in the way, and if I'm not careful, I allow my mind to stay in places that are not healthy. Then my mind is so crowded with those unhealthy thoughts that I can't hear the still, small voice of Jesus telling me to come to him when I'm weary and burdened.

This tendency of mine was highlighted for me when Myron was preaching a sermon on godly humility once. He was talking about Mary, the mother of Jesus, and how she quickly and readily responded to the angel telling her that she would give birth to the son of God even though she was a virgin. As I sat there contemplating all of that, it dawned on me: I am so *unlike* Mary.

I often wrestle with God when he speaks to me. Offering excuses, listing my insecurities, debating how it will affect my life.

Until something happens to break me or bend me to God's

will. I remember thinking, Oh God. That I would simply and immediately respond every time like Mary did, "I am the Lord's servant, may your word to me be fulfilled."

She understood the consequences of getting pregnant in that era outside of wedlock, yet she still immediately said yes. *Oh God, that my obedience would be so genuine and immediate all the time.*

I would save myself so much heartache.

Is there an area in your life where God is asking for obedience? Where he's simply saying, "Let go. Hand it to me." Is there a move you need to make? A relationship you need to mend? Or some situation that you need to bring to the altar of God like I had to bring Caleb's healing? Just to be clear, God is in control either way. You wrestling with it and withholding it from him doesn't make it any more yours or any less the Father's.

I pray you'd be like Mary. I pray you'd say, "Yes." I had to eventually say, "Yes," too. Many times, actually.

One time when Myron was at the facility with Caleb, I spent the day at the car dealership getting work done on our vehicle. I was sitting in the waiting room when the news came that there had been a mass shooting at a college across the country. Most of the students who died were freshmen that would have been Jacob's age.

It hit me hard when I thought about those families. We did not wake up on Saturday, August 29th, 2015, and think that would be the last time Jacob would wake up on this planet. I knew that those families were experiencing the same thing. They had no idea that this was their child's last day on this earth.

I closed my eyes and prayed for those families and the nightmare that was coming for them. I prayed they would find comfort in the Lord like we had.

It reminded me of a conversation I'd recently had with a newly grieving mom:

> She was telling me about crying all the time and being embarrassed because sometimes she just couldn't control it. It hurt too bad.
>
> "I remember those days well," I told her. "There were times I would go into Jacob's room, especially his closet where I could still smell his scent, and sit on the floor weeping. Or I'd pass his high school and start bawling."
>
> I continued, "Not long after the accident, I went to the wholesale club where Jacob and I used to go together often for the protein powder he used in his weight-loss plan. As I went into the store, I automatically turned left like we always did, and then it hit me all over again. Jacob is gone. I don't need his protein powder anymore. I barely made it back out to my car before the crying turned to ugly blubbering."
>
> My new friend asked me, "Does it ever get any easier?"
>
> I thought for a minute before slowly nodding and saying, "Yes, it does. I still miss him something fierce. I still grieve for all the time we won't have with him. Sometimes it still overwhelms me when I dwell on it too long. But I think I've finally come to the place where I've accepted it. I know he's with Jesus and I will see him again. And I know that Jacob loved life and fun and would want us to do the same. I'm not saying I've mastered that at all. I'm still a hot mess but I continually release my pain to God, over and over again. And it helps."

At the rehab facility each night, one of the guys from our church family would come to visit Caleb and relieve Myron so that he could go home, catch some sleep, and go to work the next day. Just like he had done for over a month with me when I was in Gainesville for the radiation treatments, he was now doing for our son.

I've heard Caleb talk about how humbling it was to admit that he needed others for *everything*, and I thought about those times when I was naked, or close to it, for the cancer tests or radiation tattoos. I would watch as Caleb, who is also very modest, was poked, prodded, and turned. I knew the embarrassment and the humiliation, and my heart would break for him.

Even in the middle of all those struggles, I was grateful for the flashes of humor. Our family has always been fun loving, and I could begin to see some of that returning. Sometimes it was just finding the little things to smile about. Other times it was distracting ourselves with a funny story. Sometimes it was a spark of Caleb's witty banter back and forth between us or the staff.

Those times were so good for me because it reminded me that our son was still here. Still battling. Still fighting. There were times when I was afraid that he would give up and not press through the stiff joints and atrophied muscles and learn to move again.

But he didn't give up. Like Mary, like me, Caleb said *yes* to the future God had for him.

I prayed he would continue to fight.

Be patient. God is the master of healing—
of putting broken things back together again.
—Pastor Ron Meyer (handwritten note in
Jenny Leavitt's Bible, December 13, 2015)

GRIEF CLUB

THE FALL OF 2015 CAME and went, and as Caleb progressed, we were able to get out a bit more. One time, we were all out for a ride when I commented to the guys, "Right after the accident, I couldn't imagine living the rest of my life without Jacob. Now it's been sixteen weeks." There was a long, silent pause as they processed my words.

It was proof that life goes on, like it or not.

Myron and I were blown away by God's provision for us after the accident. People from around the world were sending us cards and money. Local churches took up special offerings to help us while some of our sister churches covered everything from rental cars for family that flew in to providing us with hot meals each day for weeks. As the bills came rolling in, all our needs were met. Above and beyond met.

As I've mentioned, my coworkers donated four months of leave days so that I could be with Caleb in the inpatient rehab facility each day. People I didn't even know generously gave up their sick days for me.

Myron and I tie that blessing back directly to us being faithful through the years with our tithes and offerings—no matter what was going on in our lives.

A friend of mine also pointed out that people wanted to bless us like we'd blessed them in the past. She said, "You guys always take care of everyone else. Let us return it to you now."

Because of their generosity, I was able to be with Caleb, which was a godsend because between the C-collar, the broken right arm, the broken left leg, and broken tailbone, he was extremely limited in what he could do. He could not even sit up on his own, let alone go to the bathroom or bathe.

When my independent, strong-willed son, would tell me repeatedly how sorry he was that I had to help him do these things that he was unable to do, I would tell him over and over again that I wouldn't have it any other way. Not only am I his mom and I love him, but I know what it's like to be embarrassed. I know what it's like to have to depend on others because you are physically unable to do it yourself. I know what it's like to have no choice but to give up your modesty to get well.

I heard a preacher once talk about a trip to Tokyo where he first saw a form of art called Kintsugi. He explained that the Japanese take broken pottery that would normally be thrown away or cast off and instead take all those pieces and glue them back together. What makes this art so valuable is that they add flecks of gold to the adhesive. So, when they repair it, the broken lines become the glory of the piece. The value is in its brokenness that has been restored. I prayed that, in a similar way, God would do that for Caleb, and for each of our broken and damaged lives.

We had scare after scare with Caleb during that time too. He developed a bad bed sore on the back of his head that threatened to go septic. He was still battling dangerous blood clots and trying to heal from the massive trauma to his body. He began experiencing horrible GI problems due to his liver malfunctioning. He had to be hospitalized twice again through the emergency room for fever, pain, and undiagnosed issues that cropped up.

I would sit vigil next to his hospital bed, pouring out my grief and anxiety in my journal. I have pages full of my questions, despair, and grief—right alongside my hope, recentering, and gratitude. Some are smeared from dried tears, but they are evidence of my fight to overcome what threatened to take me out.

It amazes me how many times I've shared those intimate details with other grieving moms who have said how much it helped them. It also amazes me how many times Myron has shared his story about his back, job loss, and our subsequent financial catastrophe, and God has used it to encourage others that God will see them through too. And I can't even begin to count how many times I've shared my battle with cancer to a newly diagnosed friend or acquaintance in the hope of being an encouragement. I survived—you can too.

I've learned that nothing is truly lost in God's kingdom. I believe that Scripture is true and that one day, our Savior will redeem, restore, and renew everything we've ever lost. From the "big" things like a new earth that is not marred with sin to the "small" things, like restoring Jacob to us in the coming kingdom.

Pastor Joe Campbell and his wife Connie know the pain that we have experienced because they lost their fifteen-year-old daughter Gale over forty years ago. We've watched them over time as they express their grief, but also their joyful hope and longing for reunion one day. I was talking to Connie one time about it and asked her how long it had been since their accident. With tears in her eyes, she said, "Thirty-seven years. Sometimes it still feels like yesterday."

Wow, I thought. That comforts me to know that her mother's heart still grieves all those years later. I'm not weird or abnormal. Yet, she seemed so strong too. I asked about that. "How do you do it? How did you go on?"

She told me, "Sometimes Joe and I will sit out on the front porch together at night and talk about the what-ifs. What if she had lived? Would she be married and have given us grandkids by now? We'll talk about it for a little while, but we can't stay there. It's not good for us."

On the way home from church that night, I told Myron and Caleb what she said. I think we've all tried to keep that mindset since. We remember and even dream a little, but if we, if *I*, stay in that place too long, it takes an emotional toll on me. This, in turn, affects my relationships with others, especially the one closest to me, Myron.

Even after 2015 closed out, there were still more "firsts" to contend with. The first birthday—which would have been Jacob's eighteenth.

I found this journal entry I made that day:

> *November 25, 2015*
>
> *Well, Lord. Today's the day. Eighteen years ago today, you gave us Jacob Nathanael Leavitt. I am so grateful Lord. And yet, it still seems surreal that he's not here. Can you please tell him happy birthday for me? And please give him a great big hug from me too, Lord.*
>
> *Jacob—I love you so much, son. And I miss you so much that I can't even put it in words. I am so grateful that the Lord chose me to be your mom. I miss you so much. I miss your sense of humor. I miss your big, kind heart. I miss our walks and our praying together. I miss spending time with you, even in the everyday things like driving home together or listening to the radio together.*
>
> *Dad and Caleb miss you too. We're going to the cemetery today. Your headstone's in place and Caleb hasn't been there yet. I think you would like it. We used a line—the last line— from your writing on it and the best of your senior pictures. Please give Jesus a great big hug and let him know how grateful I am for what he did for us and that he redeemed you. That's how I <u>know</u> I will see you again, son. I really can't wait until the day I see you and Jesus FACE to FACE. Oh, what a day of rejoicing that will be.*

The very next day was our first Thanksgiving without Jacob. Caleb and I were talking about it sometime later and we remembered how we initially planned on flying to Idaho for Thanksgiving that year, but Caleb was still in a wheelchair, and we were not physically able to do it. We were still adjusting to using a sliding board to move him from the wheelchair to a vehicle or a chair; his mobility was still severely limited, and his pain was still great.

I remember telling the guys, "I can't do Thanksgiving like we always have this year. I don't know if I'll ever be able to do it like that again."

My mind filled with memories of crowded tables full of laughter, food, and games with friends and family before we moved outside for a game of football and later a bonfire by the pool. My shattered heart couldn't bear the thought of the empty place at the table and the forced happiness when I wanted to weep instead.

A friend of ours knew of a family in Florida who had lost their fourteen-year-old son in a similar accident just eight months before we lost Jacob and had been encouraging us to meet them. They were strong Christians—and were still reeling from their own loss. We had spoken over the phone, but when they offered to meet us at a restaurant on Thanksgiving Day, we decided to do it.

After *six hours* at the restaurant, we all realized that this was the start of a new friendship. We are so grateful that the Lord brought Albert, Yolie, and Veronica Martinez into our lives. Yolie told me that another grieving mom told her, "Welcome to the club. It's a very elite club—this club of parents who have lost a child. No one wants to join and few on the outside understand the pain."

Myron has told people:

> Sometimes you can feel like your life has been shattered into pieces. No matter how badly your life has been broken, God still wants to use you. There is a world of people out there who are in various stages of brokenness. Some a little, others a lot, but a person who has experienced bro-

kenness can truly empathize with another who is enduring it. The brokenness, disorientation, confusion, depression, dejectedness, hopelessness, all are experienced every day by millions of people, and they need someone who can empathize with them.

My wife and I have been able to walk alongside other couples who have experienced cancer because we've been through it too. We've also been on the receiving end in our own brokenness. We met our dear friends Albert and Yolie Martinez because they chose to reach out amid their broken hearts over the loss of their son in January 2015 to a drunk driver. They have shown us God has promised to rebuild, repair, and raise those who have been broken.

In many ways, we are not useful until we are broken.

God doesn't give us what we can handle.
God helps us handle what we are given.
—Plaque Caleb bought when he was still
in a wheelchair after the accident

JACOB'S LEGACY ENDURES

BY GOD'S GRACE, WE MADE it through Jacob's eighteenth birthday and Thanksgiving. Even though Caleb was still in a wheelchair most of the time, we decided to fly out to Idaho to spend Christmas with the family.

Caleb remembers, "That was still challenging because I had to be in a wheelchair all the time, even at the airport, going up the ramps since I wasn't able to walk yet. I remember how the plane trip really hurt my backside."

That was when we realized that this world is not very handicap friendly, even though they may say it is. I can't count how many times he got jostled and almost fell out of the wheelchair because of uneven ramps or sidewalks. I can't even imagine the pain he must have been in while still recovering from the surgery to place three pins in his tailbone.

While it was wonderful to spend Christmas with family, even that felt surreal. Jacob should have been there. As a matter of fact, that's exactly what Caleb said as his twenty-first birthday approached in March of 2016. He told me, "It's just weird. Jacob's not here. He won't ever have a twenty-first birthday."

He added, "I don't want to celebrate my birthday. I don't want to do anything."

He talked with his dad about it and Myron told him, "I understand, son. But other people want to celebrate you. You're alive."

Eventually, he came around to the idea and we had a party to celebrate.

By that time, Caleb had graduated to a cane and then, our stubborn, strong-willed, fighter son was walking all on his own, just like he told the doctor he would.

The doctors informed us that he would not be released to return to the job he had prior to the accident as a teacher's aide in a special-needs classroom at the local high school. Part of his duties required him to lift and assist the students, one of which was over three hundred pounds. We were told that he might never be able to return to such a physically challenging job.

At a crossroads, Caleb took time to prayerfully consider his next steps and decided to return to college. He had already received an associate degree before the accident and decided to go back for his teaching degree. He has since graduated and is teaching in the same school district that he worked at before.

It soon became apparent that I needed to return to work too. I battled guilt, regrets, and worry over leaving him at home while I was at work. Even though he was doing online college classes and was healing better than the doctors had projected, I still worried over his emotional state and the time alone. We had been discussing the possibility of getting a dog, so off to the pound we went.

There's a reason why the old saying is, "Dogs are a man's best friend." Buddy was a gift from God and quickly became an integral part in healing our wounded hearts. I'm glad he can't talk, because I'm sure he would have some stories to tell of tears, anger, and frustration. But it was such a blessing to come home and have someone excited to greet us. He became my new walking partner too.

Overall, Caleb's physical healing was going well. He was able to start driving again, which helped, as he was still in outpatient physical therapy several times a week. For other follow-up visits, I would take time off from work to go with him.

Once, he had an all-day test with neurology for the long-term effects of the traumatic brain injury. The results showed that he has some word-finding problems and some short-term memory issues. We were informed that it could take two full years for his brain to heal.

Of course, the family that we are, we tease him that the short-term memory problem will come in handy one day when he's able to say to his wife, "Oh, did you ask me to take the trash out? I don't remember you saying that."

In addition to Caleb's birthday, the spring of 2016 brought an invitation for us to participate in Jacob's class's baccalaureate and graduation ceremonies. Myron had been in communication with the principal throughout the school year and was invited to speak at the baccalaureate. It was bittersweet to watch as Myron poured out his heart to Jacob's peers.

After he expressed our appreciation for the invitation and reminded the senior class just how much Jacob loved them all, Myron shared the story of our family's loss. He also went on to challenge the group about how the decisions they make can change lives forever.

I was so proud of him as he endeavored to honor Jacob's wish that we do not give up on his generation—but reach out to them with the hope of Jesus.

Myron said, "My family's hope through all of this was that Jacob was a Christian and loved God with all of his heart. No doubt he had his struggles and difficulties, but he seemed to be able to get that all worked out."

He was then able to share the poem that Jacob had written, "Holding Me," explaining how it had been written just a short time before Jacob stepped into eternity.

Myron continued, "Jacob would want me to share with you that the decision to give your life to Jesus and serve God with all of your heart far outweighs any other decision. God is so good and wants to help you through all of life's struggles. Many people have told us how strong we have been through all of this, but I can tell you tonight, it is not our strength that has helped us through, only God's amazing grace and power."

It was difficult to hear Jacob's name the next night at graduation—but comforting to know that he was remembered.

The baccalaureate speech that Myron gave was the first of many times that he would boldly tell our story. He has said, "My theory is that if the devil's going to take one of my sons, folks are going to hear about it, and God's going to use it for good."

While Myron has spoken of our story in many of his sermons and in many different church settings, he mainly shares our story in events involving students and young people. He's spoken at Mock DUI events put on by the local sheriff's department for high school seniors before prom. He's spoken to after-school clubs and organizations at several different high schools. He's spoken at Teen Challenge, where he saw over forty young men respond to an altar call to give their lives to Christ.

That was an especially anointed message. Myron said,

> Jacob died of a broken neck and a broken back, but Jacob was so much more than a victim of someone else's bad decisions. He was seventeen years old, a senior in high school who loved football, and was a straight A student, enrolled in AP classes.
>
> Everyone loved Jacob. He was funny, clever, and extremely intelligent. He was devoted to his friends, loved his family, loved the Jacksonville Jaguars, and most of all, Jacob loved Jesus.
>
> I want to urge you—don't waste your life. Don't settle for second best. Don't go through life just existing, coping, getting by. You are not put here to just get by. God made

you for a reason, for a mission, for a purpose. That starts by asking the question, "Is this the best use of my life?"

Because there is no middle ground. The decisions that we make today determine our tomorrows.

We are always amazed at how God sets up these encounters and opportunities. It is further proof that even with our imperfections, failings, and turbulent grief, our God can take those broken pieces and create something beautiful with it—like the Japanese art.

I think of all the stories in Scripture that tell us about God using whatever someone already has in their hands.

Moses had a rod.

David had a slingshot.

The widow had a little oil.

All God asks for is that we yield the little that we have to him, then he steps in and does the rest for his own glory.

Comments from "at risk" students who heard Myron speak in November 2020:

> The most helpful thing that happened today was getting closer to God. I've done a lot of bad things and had no time to make up or correct them. Today, now, I feel different and better. I know I can walk out that door now with a better life and with a smile on my face. I know now that my mother loves me, my family loves me, and I love them too. I have great friends that make me laugh. I do my best to make them laugh and smile. Just trying to change my life around.
>
> I learned that life is short, and your choices affect everybody. Tomorrow isn't promised so forgive people."
>
> Don't drink and drive.
>
> What I learned is that you never know when your time will come. Forgive people no matter what they do.
>
> I learned that you cannot make a bad choice and then take it back. You have to live with it.

FIND HEALING

TRAGEDY HAS A WAY OF bringing clarity, transforming the blurry into focus. Any sudden, jarring event can do that—a car accident or a health scare like COVID. Whatever character flaws and relationship cracks that were present before the event will be magnified as our past hurts play right into our present problems.

Whatever coping mechanism was in place before tragedy is what we tend to revert to as well. Distance in a marriage? That will be magnified. Unhealthy emotional attachments? Porn addiction? Whatever our issue is, Satan will use it to wedge apart relationships and see if he can get us to define our spouse, our friends, whoever, as "the enemy." If we're fighting each other, we can't stand together.

I didn't know this as we approached the one-year mark of the accident. When I received the news that they wanted to schedule Caleb's court day for the exact same day as the anniversary, I lost it. Myron and I had an explosive argument over it. I flipped out and told him, "I can't do it. I can't learn Caleb's fate on the same day we mourn Jacob."

Tension was high as we tried to navigate through those uncharted waters. That was our first big fight since the accident, and after we both calmed down, I realized how much pressure Myron was under to lead our family through all of this. He had already tried to move the court date and not been successful. So when I made those comments, he took it as a personal attack, even though mentally, he knew that was not the case.

The poor communication skills we'd had before the accident carried over and were magnified in the midst of the pain and grief. Caleb wasn't faring much better—picking fights with us (mostly Myron) over nothing. But things changed for him after he went to see a counselor.

Caleb told me, "The first time I went, I didn't want to be there. You didn't *make* me go, but I knew that if I didn't, you'd keep on pestering me. So, I went thinking, *I'm just going to sit here and not say anything. It's not going to help anyway.*

"She was talking to me about some totally unrelated stuff, and I was giving her short answers like, 'Whatever.'

"Finally, at the end of the time, I asked, 'Are you going to ask me about the accident? Isn't that what I'm here for?'

"In my head I was thinking, *That way I can go home and tell Mom that, 'Hey, we talked about it. I'm good.'*

"She said, 'No.'

"I said, 'Then what am I doing here?'

"She said, 'We can't get to that unforgiveness until we talk about why you won't forgive your dad and God.'

"I said, 'What? I'm not angry toward Dad or God.'

"She said, 'Okay. I'll see you next time.'

"I got up and left, but it was eating at me, you know? Each time after that, I could tell that the counselor prayed and knew what she was doing. She would always bring it back to God, saying things like, 'I was praying for you and God spoke to me,' or, 'God revealed this to me.' Or, 'God brought this Scripture to mind. I don't know if it connects,' and then she would read it to me. On the outside, I would tell her, 'Oh, thanks.'

"But on the inside, I was thinking, *Oh, man. What is going on? That really does apply to what I'm going through right now.*"

I asked Caleb, "Have I ever told you about the first time I met with her? I came home and told your dad, 'Oh my gosh. This woman read my mail.' We were just talking, getting to know each other, and she said, 'So, which one of your parents is an alcoholic?'

"We weren't even talking about that. We weren't even talking about my childhood at all. I was like, 'Um, my mom. Why?'

"She said, 'You display several characteristics of an adult child of an alcoholic.'

"I said, 'Oh, well, all right.'"

I told Caleb, "In a similar way to you, we had to work through some of those issues before we tackled the grief issues. But in a way, as I worked through those issues, it helped the grief, too, if that makes sense."

How much of my life is viewed through the lens of my past experiences? How skewed is my processing of the painful parts because of deep wounds I've never addressed? Words of rejection spoken to me as a child . . . endless striving for perfection for trite, fleeting words of praise? My insecurities, failures, shortcomings— all of it viewed through a warped lens of my past experiences.

I thought of one of the things Pastor Joe Campbell says frequently: "How you process life is everything."

I thought of how I'd blown up at Myron over the court date—something he had not arranged and had little control over. And I realized that if our marriage was going to survive, if everything we'd been through was going to mean anything, then I had to learn how to communicate in more healthy ways and not continue in the destructive ones.

I couldn't keep protecting the wounded areas of my heart, whether it be from insecurity or thinking the other person wouldn't understand- and expect the vicious cycle to stop. Tempers would continue to flare and words would continue to be misconstrued.

After losing Jacob and walking alongside Caleb through

months of recovery, there were times we simply had to say, "We're going to fight for our marriage. We will survive. We will not die on this battlefield."

My challenge to you, dear reader, is to take stock of your wounds and hurts. Ask how many of those you've allowed healing to enter into. Because if it's not all of them, I am living proof that they will come back to haunt you. Maybe you need professional counseling, maybe you need a conversation with a pastor, or maybe you just need a long talk with the Father.

Either way, get the help you need on *this* side of grief. Because, though you may not lose a child, life is littered with hurts and disappointments. The more you find healing today, the less likely you are to operate out of dysfunction tomorrow.

> *Most marriages don't survive the death of a child*
> *because someone doesn't process it right.*
> *If you cannot leave things with God,*
> *there will always be casualties.*
> *Your relationship with God has to be*
> *greater than the tragedy.*
> —Jacob Leavitt's notes from Pastor Joe Campbell's
> sermon, "The Goodness of God" (5/14/2012)

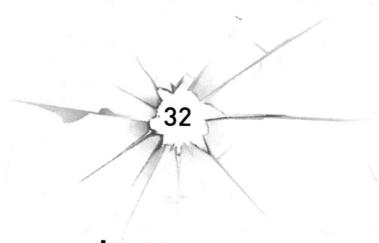

INNOCENCE

AFTER OUR BLOWUP, MYRON PUSHED our attorney to move Caleb's court date from August 30, 2016. Thank God, the courts finally agreed to move it to mid-September.

Caleb had a perfect driving record prior to the accident, but he'd received three speeding tickets since then. The judge sternly warned him to slow down and then proceeded to work through the details of the case and call for the witness. We were relieved, but not surprised, when the witness did not show up.

The outcome was bittersweet, as the judge dismissed everything in Caleb's favor. We were overjoyed to know that Caleb would not be charged with his brother's death and the court proceedings were over. In a way, we were able to close that chapter in our lives.

But that did not bring Jacob back.

We had to continue to navigate forward through the minefield of grief. That meant we needed to establish new traditions and new ways of healthy coping if we were going to be victorious and not allow this to define us forever. Fun-loving Jacob would not have wanted that.

I asked Caleb what he remembered about that day in court and he said, "Honestly, I don't remember much about it. I told Dad afterward that all I could think about the whole time was how angry I was at the other two guys across the room. At that time, I wanted to hurt them. I was still so mad."

That made me think of one of Myron's sermons where he said,

> This scene we're living in is no sitcom. It's a bloody battle.
>
> We are now in the late stages of the long and vicious war against the human heart. I know—it sounds overly dramatic. I almost didn't use the term "war" at all, for fear of being dismissed at this point as one more in the group of "Chicken Littles"—Christians who run around trying to get everybody worked up over some imaginary fear to advance their political or economic or theological cause.
>
> But I am not hawking fear at all. I am speaking honestly about the nature of what is unfolding around us . . . against us. And until we call the situation what it is, we will not know what to do about it.
>
> This is where many people feel abandoned or betrayed by God. They thought that becoming a Christian would somehow end their troubles, or at least reduce them considerably. No one ever told them they were being moved to the front lines, and they seem genuinely shocked at the fact that they've been shot at.
>
> Hello? That's what happens in war—you get shot at. Haven't you noticed with what deadly accuracy the wound was given? Those blows you've taken—they were not random accidents at all. They hit dead center. The wound is too well-aimed and far too consistent to be accidental. It was an attempt to take you out—to cripple or destroy your strength and get you out of the action.
>
> Do you know why there's been such an assault? The enemy fears you. You are dangerous big-time. If you ever really got your heart back, lived from it with courage, you

would be a huge problem to him. You would do a lot of damage . . . on the side of good.

Remember how valiant and effective God has been in the history of the world? You are a stem of that victorious stalk.

And then I thought about the night I had a dream that was so real, so vivid, that it made me weep. But with longing, not remorse.

The dream itself wasn't bad. Jacob was alive and we were doing normal, mundane, everyday life. The horrible part was waking up to the sharp pain of reality—Jacob was gone.

There is no normal, mundane, everyday life anymore.

And there never will be again because Jacob is not with us anymore.

Now, if we want to move forward and not stay stuck in our grief, we must find a new normal. A new way of doing everyday life.

Myron woke up to my quiet sobbing and asked me what was wrong. He held me close as I wept in his arms and shared the pain. Words don't do justice to how much I needed that reminder that I'm not alone. Myron knows my pain, too, and though I know I frustrate him sometimes, he's stayed.

He told a group of us in Bible study one time that he hopes to show me he loves me by making sure I'm happy, secure, and comfortable in life and that he loves me the way Christ desires.

Myron and I are not high-flying super Christians or anything. Just two people who try to keep Jesus first and then try to remember to fight as a team—not against each other. Remembering that we're in this together and we're not alone, either. Jesus is holding both of us.

We recognized that God allowed our family to experience all of this for a reason. Over the years, some of those reasons have come to light, while others might not be known until heaven. Whether it was walking alongside someone who was going through cancer or financial difficulties, or maybe injury and even unspeakable tragedy. Either way, we know God can redeem all things, even the most painful experiences or the most tragic losses in life.

He can use us as GodPrints in the lives of others.

The accident served as an important reminder, though, of how fleeting this life really is. Much like after the cancer ordeal, I had a renewed zeal to live life to the fullest and savor every moment of it.

Myron told a Bible study once, "Maybe you need to say, 'Lord, change me. Draw me unto yourself in a more powerful way so that I will pursue my destiny. I will not let the hope and dream die concerning your plans for my life.'"

We try to practice what we preach, so we sold the home we'd lived in for eleven years, packed everything, and moved 135 miles away from the familiar to the unknown. Spurred by the renewed desire to make our lives count, Myron and I stepped out in faith once again to pioneer a small church plant in Sanford.

Like any other time we'd made a step of faith to rise up and do something for God, we should've known that the devil would unleash an assault to take us out, or at the very least, bring such division to our marriage that we would implode—essentially becoming ineffective to God's kingdom.

We have the things from the last generations,
NOW WE NEED TO STIR THEM UP.
Yesterday's miracles
ARE NOT SUFFICIENT FOR TODAY.
—Jacob Leavitt's personal notes from Pastor James
Rosario's sermon "Christian Atheism" (9/9/2012)

33

THE FIGHT

WE HAD JUST BARELY UNPACKED in Sanford when a telephone scam artist convinced my mom that Caleb had been arrested and she needed to send several thousand dollars to bail him out. There was so much confusion, and we couldn't get ahold of Caleb for a while, that my mind started to question if it could be true.

Myron and I were convinced it was a hoax, but my parents were determined that the man on the phone sounded just like Caleb. Worry started circling through my mind, *Could this move and the separation from Caleb have been a bad idea? Is he not handling it well?*

We finally got ahold of him, and he confirmed it was all a lie. Unfortunately, by then my parents were out all that money. Even after getting the police involved, they were never able to recover it. They waited too long to call me because the man on the phone told them not to tell us.

Caleb told them, "Grandma, if I ever call you and tell you not to tell my parents something, the first thing you need to do is tell my parents."

Around that same time, I started working at the local high school. I had only been there a few days when a student walked into the office who not only looked a lot like Jacob, but had a similar personality too. I excused myself and went to the restroom and cried, telling myself, *What have you done? Why are you working in a high school? Are you ready for this?*

All I could do was say, "Please help me, Jesus."

You know what's really amazing about the God we serve? That little heart cry was enough. My mind settled and I was able to return to work.

Shortly after that, a mom came in, disoriented, and obviously upset. As I tried to help her, I learned that her seventeen-year-old son had been killed in a car accident caused by a drunk driver three weeks before that.

If I had not been working at the high school, that encounter, and the friendship that has blossomed from it, would never have happened. She had no idea about the internal struggles I was experiencing. That was something that God orchestrated right amid my brokenness, causing me to reach out beyond myself to somebody else who was hurting.

On top of the emotional aspect of moving away from the support system that we had in place in Jacksonville, I had numerous health issues pop up, one after another.

Before we moved to Sanford, a dermatologist who was removing skin cancer from my back told me about something called a radiation arc. He said that the likelihood of developing skin cancer from the type of radiation exposure I endured increases exponentially between roughly nineteen and twenty-six years out. At the time, I was at the low end of that range, around twenty years out. He recommended that I go back to having full-body skin checks every six months. Sure enough, it seems like every time I go, they remove at least one spot to be checked.

Then came another phone call.

"Mrs. Leavitt? We've received your CT scan results. The doctor needs you to come in so she can discuss them with you."

Man, I would really like to put all the cancer stuff behind me and just move on with my life, but residual effects continue to follow me and rear their ugly head when I least expect it.

I know that Caleb has felt like that sometimes too. Like when he had to have a colonoscopy and he was only twenty-three years old. I know how frustrated I get with the long-term health issues that I must deal with, and I think I understand when he gets frustrated trying to remember a word or having to rely on alerts in his phone because of the short-term memory loss.

We were out to eat one time and Caleb was talking about how his nose didn't feel right that day. I said, "I know you probably have moved on with life and forget that you broke every bone in your face, including your nose, but sometimes it makes me wonder if these pains you have are related to that. As in, maybe it's never going to be quite the same? Remember how you couldn't even use a straw because of that for months?"

He said, "Oh yeah, I remember that. I couldn't sneeze, either. If I did have to sneeze, I had to do it with my mouth open and it hurt so bad."

So, this new phone call brought a lot of memories, anxieties, and fear to the surface.

Once again, I was heading back to the doctor to have some organs removed. I only half-joke that I wonder if, in heaven, I will get all these parts back that they keep taking out? Or do I get all new parts since we're getting a new body?

Myron heard me say that one time and replied, "Yeah, well that's not going to happen for a while." In other words, "You're not dying any time soon, so you better keep fighting."

Sometimes I get so tired of fighting. I long for the day when all things are made new.

Sometimes I lose sight that I still live in this world, and I *do* have to fight each day for myself, my husband, my son, and those around me. It's not all about me. There's so much more at stake.

I'm not going to lie, though, that phone call was rough. Lots of anxiety over another surgery and just plain weariness of this battle.

When I cried out to Jesus that morning, a still small voice whispered to me: *Gratitude. Focus on gratitude.*

Right. That has helped me before. It will help me again.

What started with the obvious things like life, a loving family, a roof over my head . . . soon spilled over into all the other things that I am grateful for. Before I knew it, something shifted deep inside me. What was turmoil just a few moments before was now re-centered. What was frustration was replaced with peace. What was dread was replaced with a knowing. A reminder that I do not walk this path alone.

I thank God that when I've done all that I can do, *I'm not alone*. Not only do I have a husband who loves me, a son who makes me proud to be his mom, and a wonderful group of dear friends and family, but I have a God who walks alongside me through it all.

He fights for me when I can't fight anymore.

So for all of them—Myron, Jacob, Caleb, and, yes, even God—I'll continue to fight.

If hell cannot stop your walk, desires, and dreams,
he will try to hinder you, or make you stumble.
—Jacob Leavitt's notes from Pastor Ron Meyer's
sermon "Hell's Hindrances" (6/16/2013)

COURAGEOUS

THE TRANSITION TO SANFORD CHALLENGED each of us in different ways.

Caleb prayed about it and decided to stay in Jacksonville. He also had to work through the emotional roller coaster of grief, anger, and unforgiveness or it would crush him.

The three of us were talking about it later and he told us that it was rough for a time, but God helped him work through it.

He said, "Not to be sappy, Dad, but I thank God for you. Now."

After we all laughed at that, he continued, "Yeah, I didn't quite like it then, but you instilled a 'don't give up' mentality in us. Sometimes, I'm trying to help people and I don't understand because they want to quit so easily. I want to say, 'It got hard. But that's life. Sometimes life is hard.' I just don't understand that your initial reaction is, 'Okay. I'm done.' I want to say, 'What? With everything?'

"But that's it. They're done. They just walk away. Even the times when I wanted to backslide and leave the church, there was something that would stop me, and it was the impact that I would have on others. I really didn't stay because of me, I stayed because of others.

"Once God helped me work through that, then I saw all the other reasons. But really, that's what kept me. The thought that, *There are others behind you, watching you. They don't need to see you be perfect, but they need to see you fight.*

"That's just not instilled in people nowadays. How do you do that without making people want to quit? I know there's got to be a balance between those two, where you can't push too hard, but you have to instill these traits somehow."

It reminded me of a shirt that Myron used to wear when we would lead the children's ministry. It said, "It's not about me. It's all about him."

I told the guys, "I wish I had known to appreciate you instilling those traits in the boys back when they were younger, Myron. I wasn't raised that way, taught that way, and didn't hear that in the culture I was around. Unfortunately, I had to learn the hard way that there were a lot of valid points in how you were trying to teach them to be men—real men who could handle adversity."

I asked Caleb, "Do you remember that time not too long ago when we came to Jacksonville for a revival service, and I sat next to you in church? The preacher was talking about Shadrach, Meshach, and Abednego when they were thrown into the fire."

Caleb said, "Yeah, I remember saying that it amazes me that they were willing to lay it all on the line, not knowing that they were going to be delivered. They even made the statement, 'Even if our God doesn't deliver us, let it be known, O King, that we will not bow down to you.' We know what happened, but they had no idea what was going to happen. They just wanted to do what was right."

He told us that some of the guys will call him when they are faced with a decision that they're not sure what they should do and he said, "It's not because I'm this great person. It's because they know that I'm going to weigh it by the standards of the Bible and tell them, 'This is what it says. Are you going to follow that, or not?'

"Relationships end sometimes when you do that. It's not that I'm better than anyone else. But I'm not going to condone certain lifestyles either. I told a friend one time, 'If it was Jacob and he was in this situation, I would have a hard time condoning that too. I love you, bro, but you're not living right.'

"From my own mistakes, I know sometimes that pain has to happen because that's what's going to pull them back in. But even if it doesn't, you were a testimony that said, 'I'm not going to go back on my principles and my standards simply because we're blood.'

"Sometimes it is lonely because you feel like you're the only one. You look at other people and you think, *You should be here with me. Why aren't you?* But then God gives me strength to do the right thing."

I told Caleb how I'd been studying the life of Joseph in my morning devotions and was reminded again how much Joseph suffered for doing the right thing. Caleb sat back in amazement and said, "You know, I think God's trying to speak to me. That's the fifth or sixth time in the last couple weeks that I've heard somebody talk about Joseph."

Caleb told us, "I was talking to a friend and telling him how some people say that I'm trying to do too much or I'm setting unrealistic standards in how I live for God. But like I told him, 'I'm not trying to do anything except live for God. I'm not doing any of this for you to view me a certain way or for the pastor.' I mean, I care what Pastor thinks because he's my pastor, but I don't live this life for him. I live it for God. So, I'm not trying to do anything but live righteously. And even then, I don't always fulfill that."

He said that he had warned another brother recently that if you keep on flirting with things that you know are going to lead you to a bad place, don't be surprised when you end up in that bad place. That's not even like a big revelation, 'Wow.' That's just common sense.

I said, "Honestly, Caleb, that doesn't even have to be in a spiritual setting. That applies to anything in life. Some of the people that we work with in the ministry, it's like, 'Oh my goodness. Your life is such a mess.' But it's because they did one thing, which led to another thing, which led to another thing. Next thing you know, ten years have passed, and they are so bound up that they don't know how to untangle the first knot, let alone the mess that their lives have become."

Caleb said, "I and one of the sisters in the church discussed this one time. She and her husband were pioneering a church in a rough area and were working with a new convert who had a lot of problems."

She said the convert would tell her about these different boyfriends she had and how she had a baby with one while the first baby's dad was in prison. Then, when he was out on parole, she got back with him and had another baby with him. Then he tried to kill somebody and now he's back in prison. So now she has babies with two different guys and one of them is in prison. And the sister in Christ was like, "What? Caleb, I just didn't even know how to help her."

Caleb pointed out that we've known other girls who left the church and did similar things and she said, "I know. And I don't understand that, either. We were raised in the same church and heard the same preaching."

He's received flak over the years when he says things like that because people think that he is trying to dig at them because he didn't make those kinds of choices. He replies, "But we're not trying to put ourselves on a pedestal. What I'm trying to say is that if you were raised in church, expect attacks from Satan.

"And secondly if you set your will—'I'm not leaving. I'm staying and I'm going to follow God's will.'—then, hey, you may come really close sometimes and do some dumb stuff, but there's going to be something inside of you that is like, 'You know what you said. If you're going to follow that and stick to that, then you can't do this.' And that's going to stop you.

"Then you face a choice—am I going to throw it all away? Or am I going to come back, be humble and say, 'I almost made a really huge mistake.' But if you set your will, God is always faithful. He'll bring it up to you again and again."

Sometimes he tells people, "I make mistakes. There are a lot of people in the church that can name mistakes that I've made throughout the years. Big ones. But when it came down to it, I just couldn't go that way. I couldn't throw it all away. Unfortunately, a lot of people have never settled that in their hearts, though."

He told a friend, "There were a handful of times when I considered leaving the church, either because of sin that I was in or because I had been hurt by somebody. Or maybe when I was hurt because somebody was talking bad about me. Or maybe something happened, and I didn't handle it right. Whatever the case, I was up against the wall where I thought to myself, *it would be much easier if I just left.*"

Then he said, "But in that moment, what had I set in place to catch me from doing something stupid that I would regret later? That once I do it, I will feel like, *That's it. I can never come back from that?*"

So, he asked this friend, "Who have you set in your life that you have given the liberty to tell you what you don't want to hear, but need to? Somebody that even if you don't call them, they are discerning enough that they will call you and say, 'What are you doing? I know something is going on with you.' They're going to tell you the truth.

"Even more than that though, have you prayed, 'God, catch me before I do something really stupid'?"

Caleb says that when people are "wowed" by our family's story, he replies, "What other option was there? What else would I do? Cower in a corner?"

So true. With the cancer—what was my other option? Give up and die? Let the cancer take me?

With Myron's back injury and our financial devastation—what other option was there? For Myron to wallow in self-pity? For us to complain to anyone who would listen?

In one of Myron's sermons, he said, "You are going to face times in life when risk and fear are staring you in the face. I believe that's why the Bible says 'Fear not' 365 times. Because I believe that God understood that we're going to have to make the decision between fear and courage every single day. That's why the first step of courage is just showing up.

"Will we have courage when all hell breaks loose in our lives?"

He then encouraged the congregation: "Go big. Go bold. Be courageous."

You will never mature as long as it's all about you.
As long as you're blaming other people,
you'll never grow up. . . . Childish thinking
is familiar and addictive.
That's why we obsess over holding
on to those mindsets.
When we get saved, the Word of God
should shape how you think.
This will be the greatest battle you face.
No experience in life is wasted if you learn.
But if you don't, you'll just keep cycling around
and around and around.
—Pastor Joe Campbell (5/6/21)

STRETCH JESUS

CALEB WASN'T ALWAYS SO RESOLUTE, so determined, to do God's will. I wasn't either, for that matter. While I was excited about the move and starting this new chapter in our walk with God, I wasn't expecting the gamut of emotions that followed. To be honest, things were rocky for me as I tried to adjust. Myron and I attempted to be gracious with each other, but we were growing increasingly frustrated, as we didn't understand where the other was coming from.

It was such a paradox for me. I honestly was excited about what God was doing in this new season of our lives. It was proof to me that he was not done with us yet. We were seeing people saved and changed by God's Holy Spirit.

We were also reminded that we are still at war. One time I stopped by to visit with a lady who had given her life to Christ, but was struggling to come out of the streets lifestyle she was living. She was FaceTiming a friend in another state and wanted me to stay so that she could ask us both a question and hear what we had to say. I could tell right away that her friend was not a believer and was determined to argue with everything I said.

She began explaining some of her hesitation with committing to Jesus and coming to church when her friend piped in, "What did I tell you about that? You start doing stuff for God and the devil will f*** with you."

She looked at me and said, "Is that true, Jenny?"

I told her, "Well, it's true in the sense that the devil is not going to be happy that he lost you and that now you are a part of God's family."

The man immediately cut me off and said, "See, I told you. You better quit this whole God and church stuff or the devil's going to start *^&*#& around with you."

I interrupted him to clarify and finish my statement by saying, "Hold on a minute. I wasn't done. It's true that the devil's not going to be happy, but it is also true that she now has all of God's promises as his daughter. Jesus said that he will never leave us and never forsake us. It doesn't really matter what happens, we have somebody walking with us and going to battle for us now."

The look on his face was priceless, as he had no rebuttal for that.

I wish I could say that she latched onto God's promises and surrendered everything to him after that, but she still struggled with doubts and all the trappings of her former lifestyle.

We found out three weeks later that she overdosed. I hope that she had taken those questions and doubts to God, and that she was ready to meet him.

There is an old saying in our church, "The devil doesn't kick dead dogs." If you're doing something for Christ, don't be surprised when opposition arises. As a matter of fact, you can take comfort in that you are doing something to combat the forces of hell.

It's interesting how cunning lions can be when they trap their prey. They hunt together by spreading out and hiding around their unsuspecting victim. One of them will roar, sending their prey fleeing. Unfortunately, the prey doesn't realize that there are other lions waiting to pounce on and devour it.

Not long after learning of that precious lady's fate, I was reading the Scripture that talks about Satan walking around as a roaring lion seeking whom he may devour, and I thought of her. She didn't even realize that Satan had roared and scared her away from the heart of God. Unfortunately, when she fled, there were other enemies just lying in wait to pounce on her.

Then I wondered, *How often do I do that?* Satan strikes fear in me and instead of running to God with those fears, I turn to other things which end up being even more deadly. Maybe not physically, maybe worse. Maybe spiritual death and eternal separation from God.

I wasn't mindful of that when we first moved away from Jacksonville. When we bought the place out in the country all those years back, it took me time to adjust. But after a while, I grew to love the wide-open spaces with brilliant sparkling stars at night not clouded by city light pollution. When we moved to Sanford, it took me a long time to adjust to going back to closed-in neighborhoods. Even walks were more challenging for me since I didn't feel as free to cry or show emotion as I prayed. It made me a lot more self-conscious of what people would think.

Maybe it's just me, but I feel a pressure to appear to have it all together; but for healing to come, you have to be able to find people with whom you can trust to open up and be yourself—people that you can confide in, and they will accept you . . . just as you are.

Part of the struggle that I faced when we moved away from Caleb and our church family in Jacksonville was the swells of grief that I thought I was past. I started to feel so distant from God, which led to a kind of apathy.

I desperately wanted passion back, but I didn't know how to

get it. I knew my faith had floundered on the rocks, even though I never stopped believing in God. I doubted that he heard or was there, because I couldn't feel him. In my head, I knew all the promises of Scripture from being a follower of Jesus for so long. But head knowledge and heart application are two vastly different things. I could believe that God is love and that he loves people—of which I am one. But applying that to me? Another story.

I started praying for that passion to return.

In all of this, Myron was also dealing with the aftereffects of yet another back surgery. We joke around that, "Growing old is not for sissies," but in all seriousness, Myron's second back surgery really wasn't for sissies. The surgeon told him, "Mr. Leavitt, your back is not going to be able to sustain further injury. Three strikes and you're out."

Yet, there he was, just days later, pressure washing our house when I came home from work. No kidding.

The stresses of that, in addition to working a full-time job and being a full-time pastor to our small church, would sometimes take its toll on him. Couple that with my health issues and, well, let's just say that we had some heated exchanges.

I know myself enough to know that when I'm weary (physically, emotionally, spiritually), it becomes all too easy to let the flesh rule instead of pursuing God and acting and speaking as his child. I should've known myself enough to recognize the clues: isolation, irritability, fatigue, feelings of hopelessness and distance from God.

One day, some insignificant word was spoken that I normally could have allowed to roll on by, but not that day. I exploded in anger. At Satan? Oh, no.

At the time, I was blind to his manipulation, his cunning deception, to divert me from the heart of the Father. I bought the lie and trusted in my feelings over the words he so graciously gave me, "Guard your heart and move forward."

I had not guarded my heart from the enemy sneaking in accusational lies, nor did I keep God's Word hidden inside to combat those lies. I certainly had not kept forward momentum going. In fact, I felt stuck. Stuck in insecurity and defeat.

So, no, unfortunately, I didn't lash out at the *real* enemy. I lashed out at Myron, turning all my frustration on him. It shames me now to think of how I have hurt him over the years by allowing nasty words to spill from my mouth to his heart. Once I cooled off, I was grieved by my actions and not only repented to God but sought Myron's forgiveness as well.

I decided to go "old-school" and write him a note like we did when we were dating. After apologizing for wounding him with my words, I drew an illustration for him that had been rolling around in my head. Remember, Jacob did not inherit his artistic ability from me, so this was no masterpiece. It was a crude, kindergarten-style drawing, but it served the purpose, I suppose.

The stick figure loosely resembled Stretch Armstrong. Remember that little plastic toy from the 1970s that delighted youngsters with its resilient, flexible limbs? You could pull until you were sure the arms would snap off, but as soon as you released it, it would rebound back to its original position and size.

My completely unprofessional, unpolished depiction of Stretch was to illustrate for Myron how I sometimes think of Jesus and our marriage. When we decided to commit our lives together and say those vows, we did so in front of God, but also in unity with him. We consciously asked him to be with us, the central part of our relationship.

Like any relationship, that has been repeatedly tested over time. Sometimes, we are quite successful in coming together in harmony. Often, though, our personalities, upbringing, stinkin' thinkin'—a host of things, really—get in the way of unity.

As I explained in my note and with my Stretch sketch, I know that when I am upset and feel defensive, I tend to flee the conflict. Yes, I need time to process. (A little slow on the uptake, remember?) But I also just need the space to breathe. I'm feeling wounded or misunderstood or whatever the perceived offense is.

Myron, on the other hand, is the opposite. It bugs him when I want to leave the room in conflict and essentially shut down.

In my mind's eye, I picture Jesus as Stretch Armstrong, right there in the center of our marriage relationship, one arm around each one of us, holding us tightly to him. When we keep things that way, everything's smooth sailing.

But when conflict arises, as it does in all relationships, I spiral out and away from Jesus and Myron. Thank God that Jesus takes those super-stretchy arms of his and reaches all the way out to where I am and gently tugs me back to Himself and to Myron, the whole time telling me, "Hey. Come on back here. Let's work this out."

I'm so grateful for a God who gets right into the thick of it with us, not in judgment or disgust, but love and mercy. Mercy. Right there in all the muck and yuckiness.

When I've made stupid, impulsive choices that have led me into trouble, the consequences are not God's fault. No, that lies squarely with me.

Yet even then, he graciously reaches down into my pain to help me. Rather than blaming him, like a lady I met in Gainesville did, or giving up on him, like so many that we have known over the years, I need to change how I process life.

If our marriage was going to survive, I had to.

Oh God. Who am I that you would speak words of life into me? That you would tell me to arise and cross over? Do you have a plan for all of this? I'm so humbled by your great mercy, Lord. I do not deserve your kindness, your precious Spirit. Nevertheless, you give your unfathomable love to me.

Thank you for being a man of your word. Just last

night I cried out to you, "Don't leave me, God!" And this morning, you tenderly whispered your promises to my heart. Thank you for knowing me perfectly and for following through on your promises. I cannot fight these battles alone. I am not enough.

But you have promised that you will not leave me, and I trust you. Thank you for patiently walking with me. Thank you for reminding me that you will continue to do so. With your help and with you by my side, I will fight. Hell will not have the last say or take away my testimony of all you've done.

Please help me—help us—to finish well.

~From Jenny's private journal

36

LOST

WHEN THE BOYS WERE IN their teens, I was the lone female in a house full of male football lovers—High school, college, and professional. All of it. I still don't understand the game very much, but I have learned a lot from watching with them.

Myron has pulled many illustrations from the experiences too. One time he said,

> I appreciate a good running back, breaking through the line, stiff-arming the opponents, and outrunning the cornerbacks. When I played football, I was the center. I snapped the ball to the quarterback on the line of scrimmage. This is where all the big bodies go to work to either get to the quarterback (defense) or the line that is protecting the quarterback (offense). There is an old football adage that says, "The team that controls the line of scrimmage usually wins the game."
>
> *Your mind* is the line of scrimmage in your life, and whoever controls the line of scrimmage controls your life. There is a heaven and a hell, a God, and a devil. And there

is a war going on for you and your mind. Why would the devil be so interested in your mind? The answer is very simple: If he can control your mind, he can control you because the mind is the control center of who we are. That's what the Bible means when it says, "For as a man thinks in his heart, so is he."

You are what you think. The devil knows if he can get us to process life, events, and thoughts incorrectly, he has won the battle.

It's easy to be a soldier in a parade. The weapons aren't loaded. No enemies are firing back. All you have to do is keep in step. But when you're in a war, your weapons better be loaded. The enemy is always near, and you better do everything you can to stay alive and win the battle.

That's where I found myself a while later when I'd driven back up to visit Jacob's grave for his twenty-third birthday. On the spiritual battlefield.

It had been quite some time since I'd visited. It was hard for me to believe that it had been five years since I'd seen his smiling face.

It had also been a long time since I had a good cry. An agonizing, soul wrenching cry that freed something within my soul. Crying out from the depths of who I am to the only One who can change anything, who can do anything about this.

Crying for all I've lost.

Crying for all my sin.

Crying for all I'm thankful for.

Crying for all that I have.

Crying because I'm forgiven.

For the first time since the accident, I'd felt like taking a walk around the cemetery. Maybe because it was a beautiful fall day. Maybe because I've missed the walks Jacob and I used to take. Maybe because I missed the Father—the way we used to talk when I would walk.

Remembering the times of laughter and joy, heartache and pain, and everything in between, I meandered the paths. Lifting my eyes, I saw the graves of thousands upon thousands—no, millions upon millions—who have died and stepped into eternity.

> Oh, God. If losing one son hurts my heart this much, I can't even imagine how much your heart is shattering over all your children that are separated from you. Some of them lost forever.
>
> What kind of stories would they tell? What kind of hardships did they endure? What happy experiences did they enjoy? Is anyone remembering them right now? Wishing they were here to have and to hold?
>
> I looked at my own life and thought, Who am I that you should see? That you should care that I'm hurting?

It's much easier to avoid the pain. If I could read a good book, find comfort in food, stay busy, or whatever else I use to avoid the piercing pain, then maybe I would refrain from poking the tender places of my grief. Maybe then I could go on with life.

As I continued to wander the cemetery, I saw another woman and another grave. She'd thought to bring a blanket to lay over the grave she was at so she could sit down without ants crawling on her. As I walked past, I turned my face away to give her privacy. How weird is it that it felt good to know that I was not alone in my grief? That others were hurting too?

Someone once asked Billy Graham, "What has been the greatest surprise of your life?" He answered, "The brevity of it."

Standing in a cemetery filled with tangible reminders of that brevity, I remembered something Myron once said. "Every day needs to count. Time is passing by, and we don't want to squander this precious thing God has given us called life. It is not enough to do well for the first five years or the next twenty years in this race of life. We must finish well too."

I wondered how many graves were filled with the shells of people who felt as if they'd finished well. How many had lived to make every day count—hanging on to those GodPrint moments when times got tough, keeping them in the faith? I believed Jacob had.

That reminded me of another story that I'd heard. Two men were talking about making the most out of life and the younger asked the older for any words of wisdom. The elderly man said, "I think of life as a wheelbarrow full of precious gems. Each gem is an allotment of our time, and the longer I live, the more gems leave my wheelbarrow. I only have a few gems left now and I want to make each one count."

Oh God, I thought, I want my gems to count too.

I approached a crossroad. To my right, a funeral was about to begin, so I turned left. After a few more minutes, I realized I was lost.

I'll just cut through these hedges; My car is on the other side of them.

I was wrong. Had I deceived myself into thinking I knew where I was? That I could find my way out of the twisting path I was on?

I did the only thing that I knew to do. I went back to what was familiar. To what I knew to be the right way.

What do you know? When I got back to that spot and turned my head in the other direction . . . just around the bend . . . there.

Jacob's grave, with the birthday balloon flapping in the wind.

A small, quiet whisper across my soul reminded me that when I'm lost and wandering aimlessly, maybe even *thinking* I'm going the right way, if I just hold on to him, then what I'm really looking for is right around the bend.

I just can't see it yet.

God, where are you? I'm trying to do what's right. I'm trying to still trust you. But it's so hard when I don't feel you. When I can't feel your presence. When I can't feel anything. How do I get through this?

Who could I talk to? I should be further along than this. I should be over this, right?

Beyond this point in the grief.

~From Jenny's private journal

37

SHOCK AND AWE

MYRON AND CALEB ARE BOTH strong-willed, and they clashed a lot as the boys were growing up. So, it didn't surprise me when Caleb said the counselor told him he needed to work through his anger toward his dad and God before anything else. I'm grateful for a Christian counselor who would speak the hard truths and pray too. And I'm grateful that Caleb chose to continue to receive the hard truth and do the work to let it change him.

He told me,

> I began to see the way that I was viewing Dad and how it was coming out in my actions. I would think that he was responding in a certain way when he wasn't. But that was my skewed perspective and view of him.
>
> I think that was a yearlong process. I remember the week when it finally broke though. In 2017 when we were at a Bible conference, two men preached on bitterness and forgiveness and it was like a one-two punch. I was slowly trying to work through the anger, but then something else

would come up and hit me again. Or Dad would do something, not even knowing what was going on inside of me, and the fiery darts would come to my mind. *See, he is this way.* One of the major things was when I was going back to work. I was scared because I'd been out for over a year. I was scared to get back into real life.

He said that his dad did the right thing and challenged him to get back into it. He told me,

But it was also the fact that he left the decision to me. In fact, both of you said that if I wanted to not work and focus on school, continuing in that full time, that was fine. But to me, because I was viewing it a certain way, it was like a backhanded thing to where I felt like both of you, but mostly him, didn't think I could do it. I look back now, and it doesn't make any sense, but whenever you're living every day in bitterness and anger, everything is tainted and twisted in a way that it's not, but you don't see it until you're out of it and look back and say, 'Wow, I was really twisted.'

I know there were things growing up that happened, but Satan always takes at least a little bit of truth—maybe even half of what he's saying is true—to plant those seeds. I realize now that I was weak spiritually. In that moment, whenever you let bitterness fester, it weakens every other part of your spiritual being. I wasn't really fighting.

That week at conference though, seeing you guys still choose to go out to pioneer a new church again, in the midst of everything else, it was like something broke inside of me.

It was crazy to me when I realized the week after that, I'm not bitter anymore. I'm not bitter at God. I'm not bitter at Dad.

He said he's told people since then that whenever he chose to forgive and leave what happened in the past and move forward, it was like he didn't have to make a conscious choice to forgive the two guys in the other vehicle. It was already done. It hinged upon him forgiving his dad and God.

He told me that seeing the counselor, coupled with the recovery class at church, really helped. The first time he took the class, he was still hesitant a little bit. He said he was kind of taking it in and observing. But the second time was after he had made some big mistakes. He realized that he could probably have gotten through it quicker if he had opened up more the first time through the class. The second time he was a lot more open.

It was a good thing. Another GodPrint, really, that Caleb worked through his anger when he did, because not long after that, one of the sisters in the church approached him. She had waited over a month to tell Caleb what she'd heard from a family member of the drunk driver who hit our boys because she thought to herself, *I don't know how he will respond to the news.*

She approached him after church one morning and said, "I need to tell you about a conversation I had with a family member of the guys who hit you. The lady asked me, 'You know that Ryan's dead, don't you?' And I said, 'No. You're talking about the one who hit the Leavitt boys, right?' And she told me, 'Yes.'"

Almost three years after our accident, the drunk driver who hit our kids was driving and his pregnant girlfriend was with him in the car. He was not drunk this time, but he was driving. It was late at night, fewer than five miles from where our accident had happened. A drunk driver coming the other way crossed the median and slammed head-on into them and killed Ryan and his pregnant girlfriend instantly.

It was all over the news, just like our accident had been. So, three years after our accident, the drunk driver was killed by a drunk driver. Then, almost three years after that, again, the news reported on the drunk driver that had hit Ryan. That accident was not his first DUI, so he was sentenced to sixty years.

When the sister from the church told Caleb all of this, he had to process it all for a couple of days before he called us. He told me, "I googled it, Mom. It's true. It just happened."

Another part of that story that is mind-boggling to me was that after we learned that Ryan had died, my husband went back to see the family again. We lived 150 miles away by that time, so he had to make it a point to go and try to talk to the family.

He recognized the first father right away when the door opened, but the father didn't recognize him. He asked Myron, "Who are you?"

Myron reminded him who he was, and the father said, "Yeah, I think I remember you."

My husband said, "Well, I definitely remember you. We heard about what happened with your son, and I just wanted to let you know from one grieving father to another grieving father, that there's forgiveness. There's hope."

I wasn't there when Myron had this conversation, but he told me later that the father just went on and on about how wrong it was for that driver to be drunk and hit his son and kill him.

Finally, Myron said, "I know."

He said at that point, the father stopped and said, "Oh, right."

Myron said, "Well, I just wanted to come by and speak to you for a few minutes."

It ended awkwardly as Myron left and came home.

It's sad to me when I think that maybe one of the reasons why God put it on my husband's heart to reach out to those young guys after our accident was because God knew that it wouldn't be too much longer, and that young man would step into eternity. What's sad is that father didn't let Myron talk to him the first time he went there.

Later that day, I told Myron, "I don't know. I guess I could understand a parent in that situation, not knowing what the other parent might want to say to his child, so they don't allow them the chance. But to think that maybe, just maybe, God had sent you there for that very reason. *What if.*"

I guess we'll never know.

On our very best day, we are still deserving of hell.
—Evangelist Dennis Wright (handwritten note in Jacob's old Bible)

38

Six Months of Hell

THE BATTLE RAGED AROUND ME—US, really. I would recover from one health issue to be assaulted with a ministry crisis, followed by another dramatic incident. The six months of hell started with all three of us contracting COVID.

I was scheduled to have surgery because tests showed a high chance that the gallbladder polyp that I was battling was cancerous. Myron and I went to the hospital only to be turned away because the COVID test I'd taken the day before was positive. Two days later, we were both miserable. It was bad for about a week, and we experienced about every symptom on every COVID list you've seen.

Someone told me once, "You should get a T-shirt made that says, 'I survived COVID.'"

I just nodded at him, but inside I was thinking, *Sir, you can't fit everything I've survived onto a T-shirt.*

The surgery was rescheduled and shortly after recovering from COVID, I had my gallbladder out. When I went back for the postop visit, the doctor was bewildered by the results: I had a polyp and he removed it. However, even though it had all the hallmarks of cancer, they'd run the tests twice and it came back negative. He was almost apologetic that they'd removed it.

I was so relieved to be done with the looming cancer threat that I told him, "That's okay. I'm just glad it's over."

The news made me wonder, though. I had been almost rudely bold with God before the surgery one day when battling the lingering possibility of returning cancer. I'd said, "God, you either healed me all those years ago or you didn't."

I think God not only healed me all those years ago, but he intervened in this episode too.

I'm not afraid of the cancer returning. If I'm honest, I'm weary of the ordeal that would follow a new diagnosis and all that would entail: the doctor appointments, hospitals, treatments.

While I was recovering from the surgery, we passed the milestone of the anniversary of the accident. I remember turning up the radio and singing loud and proud—by myself, in the car—to a song called "Defiant" by Rend Collective that day. The lyrics settled my resolve to not dwell in despair as I remembered what our family endured five years ago.

I'd been feeling like God was whispering to my soul, *Guard your heart and move forward.* Boy, do I wish I'd realized how much I needed to cling to that. I should've written it on every scrap of paper I could find and tacked it up where I could see it multiple times throughout the day.

Wandering from one battlefield to another, I lost sight of it. For a while, at least.

During all this, there was also civil unrest like none we've ever witnessed in our communities and nation. Who can forget the 2020 election?

While that was going on, there was a ministry crisis that Myron and I stepped in to assist with. As with any issue like that, people are the greatest concern and we tried to love and support them to the best of our ability.

Next thing we knew, the holiday season was upon us, along with Jacob's birthday. These have become easier with time, but they're still difficult.

Myron and I also had birthdays—which in themselves are challenging. Some of our best memories are family birthdays spent with fun, fellowship, and friends. Now they seem an echo of the past as we think of our missing loved ones. We all try to focus on life, gratitude, and new traditions, but they're still hard.

I was informed at my six-month dermatology checkup that I had melanoma on my back, and so that had to be removed too.

I'd also been battling sinus issues and headaches for several months—even after I had a second sinus surgery less than a year earlier. I was sent for testing and the tonsil that had not been removed years before with its twin now popped positive for precancer and needed to come out.

I had a coworker once who found out that she had cancer. She was, understandably, upset and fearful and said, "I just don't know how you do it, Jenny. I don't know how you've gone through everything that you've gone through. I think I would be curled up in a ball on my bed and never able to leave my house."

I told her, "The only way I have been able to process this life is through the strength that I have found in Jesus. I share that with you not to badger you into my faith, but so that you can have that same strength. The reality is that life happens to everyone. Life can change in a moment of time. There is nothing special about us. As we've gone through these things, we've just really tried to process things right. Sometimes when you're not sure, you just have to do the next right thing. I'll be honest with you, too many times I tried to find other ways to ease the hurt or the confusion."

I'll tell you that ever since the accident, I think I have a lot more compassion for people with addictions. Not excusing them, but I understand them a lot better now. There's so much hurt and pain, and if you don't face it right and process it, then you'll find something to at least mask it for a while.

Myron has used this illustration a lot over the years:

> Whether we realize it or not, we all long for something more in our life. I call it a hollow spot, a God-like puzzle piece that is missing. For instance, we might try to fill that with a relationship. We'll just keep trying to push that relationship into the puzzle, but it doesn't fit. We'll say to ourselves, 'I guess I'll just make it work for now, even though it doesn't really fit.' That might work for a while, until we're not fulfilled again. Then we blame the other person and say, 'You're not fulfilling me.'
>
> They are not supposed to fulfill you. That spot will only be filled by God, the one who fits that puzzle piece. I think that's why so many of our relationships are aggravating, because we're trying to make that person fit that puzzle piece, and they were never designed to do that. Only God can.

I thought, *Why do I turn to other things when I should know better?*

If I let it, shame comes. But when I bring my shame to him, I find true freedom; joy, deep down inside; relief.

So, I try not to be so quick to judge how someone has dealt with the hard knocks that life has thrown their way. We've been dealt some hard knocks, tried some things, failed, and found that there's still only one thing that is sure and true.

I was talking to the counselor one time, and she said, "Jenny, you know they call it comfort food for a reason." She told me that was one of the things that Christians battle with the most. They know that addictions and immoral lifestyles are wrong, but everybody has to eat. It becomes way too easy to soothe our hurt with food.

I have found that the only way to truly step forward in healing is to not mask the pain and the grief, but to invite Jesus into all of those hurting and wounded places.

I told my friend that day, "You know, it's kind of silly how we think we're hiding these things from God. It's like mentally we know that he sees it all, but we're hoping to keep this part hidden because we're so ashamed. He's a gentleman, and even though he's waiting at the door, he won't barge in without being invited. But the only way to really get any healing is to open the door and let him in. Let him see all the ugliness that's in there."

She was still listening, really listening, so I continued, "I get it. I totally get the battle with the despondent feelings, the uncertainty, the anxiety. The only thing I can say is that I have found that the only thing that gives me peace is going back and doing those things that gave me peace before. With everything that Myron and I have gone through, it's still the basics of Christianity—just staying connected to Jesus."

My friend didn't give her life to Jesus that day, but she's asked me a lot about him since then.

You know what else I've discovered? That if God is willing to offer me grace, forgive me, help me to stand back up, dust me off, and give me *another* new start—then I have got to be gracious with myself. I've got to be willing to say, "Okay, so you messed up. That's not the end."

I told my coworker that day, "This is something that you can do too. You have the same Savior wanting to work in you. To be completely honest with you, you may stumble and fall some. I know I have lots of things I wish I had a do-over on. Thank God we have a Savior who will pick us up out of the pit, the junk that we get ourselves into, pull us up, and plant our feet right back on that solid Rock."

I can't count how many times over the years I've had similar conversations with all different kinds of people from all different walks of life with all different kinds of trials and difficulties: Divorce, losing someone, terminal illness, financial troubles. Sometimes the trouble was brought on by themselves. Other times it was completely out of their control.

It really doesn't matter because it's still the same Savior no matter what the trial is. It's still that same Jesus who said, "I will never leave you. I will never forsake you." It's still the same Savior who has shown up in every season of my life, leaving GodPrints as a bread crumb trail back to him, no matter how far away I'd walked.

When Peter was doing the incredible and walking on water to Jesus, it was only when he took his eyes off the Savior and started looking at the storm, the size of the waves, and the force of the wind, that he started to drown.

Similarly, when I took my eyes off my Savior and started paying more attention to my turbulent feelings in those six months of hell, I started to drown.

It's easy to act like a Christian. It's hard to react like one.
—Pastor Joe Campbell

39

ONE STEP BACK

"SHE DIED, MYRON. MY MOM died."

I was in the specialist's office when my phone rang. Once again, the news was shocking. My mom, who I talked to almost every day, had died. Peacefully, it appeared. But it still hurt my heart.

God bless my husband. Right in the middle of his workday, he offered to stop everything he was doing to drive to where I was and take me wherever I needed to go. No hesitation, no reservation. Just, "What can I do? Can I come get you?"

"No, that's okay. I'll meet you at the house as soon as possible and then we can go together from there."

As Myron walked in the door a little while later, he opened his arms and I buried my face in his chest, weeping. He held me as I cried, soothing me with his strength and presence. No words were necessary. Once again, I was reminded how grateful I am that I'm not alone in this life.

Losing my mom was difficult, but I think it was made a little easier by the knowledge that the tender places of my grief would eventually scar over. The scar would remain, like it had with Jacob, but the pain wouldn't always be so raw and vulnerable.

I can look back now and see that God was practically beating me upside the head trying to prepare me and help me be ready for that six months of hell, but I was too busy, too distracted, to see it for what it was. Over and over, he was showing me verses like Hebrews 10:35–39 and making the phrase, "We are not of those who shrink back and are destroyed," pop out at me.

Oh, how I wish I'd heeded that wisdom, done a better job of guarding my heart, and not allowed myself to get bogged down in the constant onslaught of physical and mental issues, but been more careful about what I let in and what I kept out.

While talking to the counselor about the six months of hell, she said, "Honestly, Jenny, it sounds like you have some detachment issues going on, which totally makes sense with everything that you've been going through these last six months. It's a coping mechanism when it feels like your life is just one bad thing after another. When they pile up and it can feel overwhelming, it sounds like you just kind of shut down because you couldn't take one more thing."

She said exactly what I'd experienced. "In the beginning, it probably felt like, *Okay that was bad, but I got past that.* But then, *Oh, here's something else.* But, *Okay, I got past that.* But then something else happens. One way that people cope is they just detach themselves from it all, so they won't feel overwhelmed. Essentially they shut off their feelings."

It was certainly true for me. I'd begun to feel distant—from God, Myron, and others. It was hard to pray, hard to connect with anyone. I'd finally had enough and reached out to her for help.

She went on to equate what I was experiencing to a faucet where I'd turned the flow of water off completely until I decided what I wanted to do about it all. That way I could control when I wanted to deal with the fallout.

It was going to be up to me to slowly turn the faucet back on. But that was necessary if I wanted to be healthy, which I did.

I had a choice. Did I recognize where I was at and change some things to help me move forward and overcome this? Would I make some steps to help me reconnect with the people and things that have helped me before? Reestablishing those things that I'd let lapse?

Was I paying attention to what my thoughts were and where they were coming from? Or was I living my life based on my feelings? Perhaps feeling that God was not there with me when I know that his Word clearly says that he never leaves me?

It was up to me to remind myself of who I am in Christ.

One of the sermons Myron preached in the middle of that six months of hell was about an Old Testament account of when God's remnant people were supposed to go back and rebuild the walls in Jerusalem, but they neglected to do so. That caused the city to be vulnerable to attacks of the enemy. He said, "When you know there are things in your life that you need to rebuild, and you neglect to do so, you put it off; you put other things first. Then you leave those things vulnerable to the attack of the enemy.

"Is God saying to you, 'Let's talk about these areas?'"

Like that day that I was lost in the cemetery, I had to go back to what was familiar and true if I was going to get back on a trusted path—the only trusted, tried, and true path of life there is.

I don't always walk in it, but thank God, I know where to go to find it again. I felt like a contender in a boxing match against an unseen foe who was pummeling the life out of me. Spirit battered and bleeding, I lost sight of that precious lifeline God provided to me before the assaults began.

The tension in our marriage seemed to increase with each new challenge too. That dream from not long ago came to mind and exposed the spiritual battle raging all around us, over us, for us. For *me*.

Satan knows he can't have me. I belong to Jesus.

Satan can, however, *with God's permission,* challenge all that I hold dear: Things I've committed to God over the years in the quiet, personal moments spent with him in prayer and reflection.

All of these memories flooded my mind like arrows—sharp, to the point, and in rapid succession.

Wow!

Hell really does hate us. Satan can't have me, so instead he probes my weaknesses to see exactly where the vulnerability lies and then executes a strategic plan of attack to discredit God and try to cause me to question, like Eve, *Did God really say? Does God really care?*

Or planting seeds of doubt like, "See, he can't be trusted. One after another, these things keep happening to you. And where is he?"

Satan can't have me. He can't have our marriage. He can't have our son. He can't even have our other son—he already made it home. The only weapon left in his arsenal is to discredit God in my eyes—to get me to doubt that he is trustworthy and true to his Word—Until, eventually, my mind is a littered minefield—shrapnel, and debris everywhere. I should've clung to God's warning to me like the lifeline it was meant to be.

The insight gleaned from that dream was the reminder I needed of the very real battle we were born into. The stakes are high. Life or death. Heaven or hell. Victory or defeat.

If I was going to survive, I'd have to make a renewed effort at devotions and prayer, purposing in my heart to not let the devil have a playday in my mind. I'd have to do my best to judge those rogue thoughts for what they were and replace them with truth, returning to those GodPrint moments to bind my wandering heart to him.

When my feet slipped off the rock into the turbulent waters of grief that threatened to drown me, even then he was with me. . . . Oh, God. Please forgive my unbelief. Believing the lies that you don't care. Doubting your words that you would never leave me. Putting my focus on me and my feelings . . . or even the lack of them. Thank you so much for your grace and mercy that reaches out to me and lifts me up out of the turbulent waves of grief. Planting me firmly on the Rock that is so much higher than I. Clasping me to your side, reassuring me of your love, even when I couldn't see you, feel you, or hear you, you were there.

I'm so grateful for your mercy, Jesus. Even when my wanderings took me away from you, you were faithful to me—faithful to your promises. Even in those dry, barren seasons, you were able to work things for my good.

~From Jenny's private journal

40

MAKE THAT YEAR OF HELL

I OPENED MY EYES INSIDE the back of the ambulance as the paramedic tried to find a vein to start an IV. I was relieved that he was busy and wasn't watching me as I looked around. I needed some time to calm my heart. The uncertainty of what was going on alarmed me to my core.

Just the day before I had been fine. But in the span of less than twenty-four hours, I must have thrown up over thirty times. I was so dehydrated I couldn't even keep sips of water down, let alone walk to the ambulance because my legs were cramping so bad. As my eyes took in the instruments around me, we raced out of the neighborhood to the emergency room.

My mind wandered to what it must have been like in the back of the ambulance the night of the accident. I'm so grateful for those first responders who feverishly worked over Caleb to keep him alive.

The paramedics suggested taking me to the closest stand-alone emergency room because the Delta variant of COVID had flooded our local hospital and they were concerned I'd be waiting for hours just to be seen.

By that time, I was hurting so much and I was so dehydrated, I didn't care. I just wanted to know what on earth was going on.

The emergency room team sent me for a CT scan and worked to curb the pain and dehydration while waiting for the radiologist to read the scan.

The news was not good and totally unexpected. My abdomen was a mess and they needed to admit me. While waiting for transport, they told me that they needed to place a tube down my nose to my stomach. I tensed immediately and considered refusing. The only other time that medical professionals had attempted that was when I had a bad reaction to the chemotherapy all those years ago. I remember the uncomfortable, miserable feeling of them trying to get me to swallow a tube that was being pushed through my nose to my stomach. I cried after they'd tried repeatedly and then they eventually gave up.

This time, though, I was determined to handle it better than I had back then.

"Okay, what do I need to do?"

It was still miserable and very uncomfortable as they forced the tube down. I won't go into the gross details but let's just say that it was very messy, but when it was over, the nausea started to ease.

They continued to give me anti-nausea meds with pain killers, and eventually I was taken by ambulance to the hospital. I could sense the stares and pitying looks as I was wheeled through the ER with the tube coming out of my nose. One lady even said, "Oh, you poor thing."

I waited in a room, all by myself, for over eight hours until a room finally opened up. The surgical team came in and I was told that I need emergency abdominal surgery to determine exactly what was going on. All they could tell for sure was that I had some kind of obstruction. Suddenly, things moved fast. After waiting so many hours, within an hour I was in the OR and they were sedating me.

I think people have a hard time believing me when I say that while the pain was great, the isolation from Myron was just as hard. Maybe harder.

Because of COVID, he wasn't allowed anywhere—not the ER, not the waiting room, not my hospital room.

I went in the ambulance with my cellphone and the clothes on my back. No charger, no purse. Nothing else.

While I was drifting off to sleep, the nurse in the OR asked, "Your husband knows about this, right?"

I said, "I was able to send him a quick message before they wheeled me out of the room, but I don't know if he got it. Can you please call him?"

She said, "Sure, sweetie. I'll call him."

I woke up later to find the tube gone, but the pain intense. Just a different kind of intense.

I wanted Myron by my side so bad that I started to cry. I felt so alone.

The medical staff was so overworked that it took three or four times longer to do anything as it had in my past hospital stays. My anxiety level started to climb right along with the pain. The post-surgery meds kicked in as the surgeon came to tell me he that he'd been able to use seven laparoscopic incisions instead of one long cut.

The mesh that had repaired an umbilical hernia years ago had moved and the hernia had ruptured again. There was also another, smaller hernia that I wasn't aware of that had wrapped itself around my stomach, causing the vomiting. The doctor said it had literally twisted my bowels and stomach up together.

On top of that, he told me that the radiation scarring was extensive and equated it to "spider webs" sticking all over my internal organs. He'd had to cut through those as well.

I had an external drain and was told that they'd need to run tests to determine if everything was "plumbed" right. If not, I'd have to have another emergency surgery.

Shortly after the doctor explained all of this, I received a roommate. She was a bitter, nasty old woman who cussed at the staff and watched violent TV.

I tried, I really tried, to pray. The anxiety was climbing, and I asked a staff member who came in if I could change rooms. That process took almost eighteen hours because the hospital was overflowing with COVID patients.

I told the nurse, "I just want my husband. Is there any way he can come?"

She said, "No, I'm sorry. Would you like me to get your cellphone for you so you can call him?" I told her that my phone was dead and that another staff member had said that I could call the operator to be connected to Myron that way. But every time I tried that, the operator didn't pick up, either.

Finally, the day after they moved me to a room by myself, a medical assistant graciously offered to let me borrow her personal charger and I was finally able to call Myron and message Caleb. There was also a nurse on that floor who treated me as a person worth his time and care. I appreciated both of them so much that I made sure to write a note of commendation to their supervisors on their behalf. When the world had gone crazy, they were kind and considerate.

One of the times that the doctor came in to check the drain, I asked him for more clarity about what had happened and if there was anything I could have done (or not done) to prevent it.

He said, "Your abdominal walls were very weakened. It's highly unusual for the stomach to twist like that. But, no, there's not really anything that you could've done or not done."

I was talking to Caleb about it later and he said, "Mom, you experienced a brief glimpse of the isolation the world has felt for the last eighteen months during COVID."

I thought, *Wow, he's right.*

No wonder the suicide and depression rates were skyrocketing. What do people turn to in times of fear, anxiety, uncertainty? Such sudden change in life's plans?

Even me, who has walked with Jesus through some horrible things and come out the other side to talk about it, sunk to some dark places. The only thing that helped cause a shift—and even that wasn't an immediate one-eighty, but more a gradual turning back to truth—was me making a choice.

I said, "Lord, where are you? What is going on here?"

Nothing. No soft whisper speaking to my heart. No warm fuzzy feelings.

I remembered how the Lord's Prayer had helped me the night of the accident, so I went line by line and did that again. It helped. A little.

I said, "Lord, Okay. I don't feel you at all right now. But you said that you would never leave me nor forsake me. So, you're here. I believe it. I don't feel it at all, but I choose to trust you."

And *that* was when I noticed a subtle shift in the darkness. I still struggled out of the despairing feelings and isolation. I want to trust God every day, all the time. I should trust God every day, all the time. He's been so good, so faithful to me—to our family.

So, it shames me to know how quickly the traumatic change shook me to my core. How it destabilized me so rapidly. It plunged me into deep, dark places I never wanted to be in again, forcing me to face the terrorizing fear of the traumatic unknown, uncontrollable events of life again that startle with their unpredictable explosion into our lives.

It all happened so rapidly I felt like I was experiencing whiplash as I struggled with questions like, "What just happened here? And, what's going to happen next? Is this something else that's going to radically change my life forever?"

Sunday night I enjoyed a great church service and then fewer than twenty-four hours later I was in the ER for some unknown, unpredicted health issue again.

One of the lessons learned along the way was that I needed to be more intentional about pausing to reflect on how I could have handled something better so that next time I would be more prepared. This became startlingly clear to me after the emergency abdominal surgery.

I'm sorry it took me so long to force my mind to slow down and reset on Christ and his promise. Yet when I consciously made the decision to do that, and that subtle shifting occurred, my mental state continued to improve, little by little. Talking openly with trusted people in my life helped as well. Focusing on the good was also a game changer.

None of those "strategies" were new to me, and I can't honestly say that I was consciously thinking of them as a strategy at the time.

But unfortunately, this wasn't my first experience with an unexpected traumatic event. In fact, that was the crux of the matter. I knew that out-of-control, dark place well. It threw me back to those dark times in my life of the cancer and the night of the accident, especially.

I know I can attribute some of the mental onslaught to Satan and his lies. He's very proficient at the arrows that he lobs into our deepest wounds. I'm not about to give him the glory for me not resisting those arrows faster.

Yet, I can also see God's grace. He did come alongside me when I reached out to him. It may not have been instantaneous, as I would have liked. Our God's not a genie waiting on our beck and call.

But he has walked with me through the valley of the shadow of death before and in the uncertainty of this time as well.

While trying to work through this latest episode in the year from hell, a friend said, "Jenny, I think you're looking at this wrong. You were plummeted into an uncertain, fearful situation, yet you advocated for yourself to move to a different room, to try to reach Myron, to get the help you needed. Have you considered that while you feel that you didn't respond correctly fast enough, it *was* faster than in the past? That's progress. You recognized the mental battle and made steps to change pretty quickly, all things considered."

When I thought about what she was saying, I realized that it *was* progress. Still, I thought, *Oh God, help my default be faith, not fear.*

No wonder Scripture tells us that we must renew our minds daily. I must be active in applying it to my own situation and to the feelings that long to control my mind, my behavior.

The struggle is real. But so is the Savior.

When I gave him that small open door of faith and said, "This is all I've got right now," he came in. Gently restoring my soul to a better place. He's so good like that.

Oh Jesus, thank you for forgiveness. Thank you for being that steady Rock that is still there—even when an unexpected hurricane is whirling around me. The Rock is not moved, though waves crash all over the top of it, though mighty winds buffet it.
YOU ARE THAT FAITHFUL ROCK.

~From Jenny's private journal

BREAKTHROUGH

"**I FEEL LIKE THE SIX** months of hell was really the year from hell, Myron. But I also feel like God's been helping me make sense of it all."

I was trying to explain to Myron the breakthrough that I'd experienced recently.

I told him, "You've heard me tell people that when I had cancer, my biggest mind battle was the boys. I finally went out in the living room and said, 'God, you've got to give me peace. I can't keep going on like this. I'm not leaving until you meet with me and give me peace.'"

That was the night that he spoke to me, 'They were Mine before they were yours. I love them more than you do and I'm going to take care of them. Whether I choose to take you home or not.'

That settled things in my heart so much that even as the boys were growing up, that peace remained with me. When other moms would be fearful of their children going to play at the park or spending the night at somebody else's house, I didn't have to struggle with that. That peace continued to stay with me. That stronghold had been broken when God met me that night.

Fast forward to the night of the accident, when we didn't know for sure that it was the boys. In the middle of all that chaos and confusion, when Myron was on the way to the accident scene and I was pacing back and forth, battling that similar fear. I finally said, 'That's enough. God, you told me all those years ago they were yours. I still trust you.'

Then we moved to Sanford, and I had that rough patch emotionally. As I've been asking God to help me process all this correctly, it's become clear to me that I think a big issue with me was struggling to place Caleb in God's hands and leave him there. Because now we are a two-hour drive away and we're not there if he needs us. God must help him.

Then, when I went through that six months of hell, I started to cry out to God for relief and help.

Over this last year, I had two startling dreams. The first one reminded me of the war we're in. The second dream, I remember the sense of weightlessness I felt. I imagine it's what astronauts feel in outer space. The lack of gravity tethering us to earth. Somehow, though, I remained well fixed in the space where I was, just out of sight of a great room.

I was looking through an arched doorway to a large throne. Somehow, I knew it was God even though I couldn't see him clearly. It was more of an internal knowing—*that's God*.

Out of the darkness came a voice. Intelligent, yet cunning. Bitter, yet also cloaked in obligatory respect, "She doesn't really trust you. Take away your tangible presence. Let her think you're no longer there—that you don't really care. Challenge everything that she thought she knew about you, and you'll see that I'm right."

I woke with a start, eyes wide open in the darkness of our bedroom. Now keep in mind, this was when I was going through that season where I was questioning, *Where are you, God? I don't feel you. I just want some passion back. What is going on?*

As I laid there, I thought, Is that my problem? Is it really a trust issue? I'm not trusting you at your word? Have I been relying on my feelings here? I'm trusting my feelings more than I'm trusting you?

I had an 'Aha.' moment and something broke. The dry season was over.

The dream was so brief that I didn't hear how the Lord responded to the allegations. Somehow, I knew that was for a reason. Because only I can answer that.

Suddenly and with clarity, the last several months made so much sense. As I began to think of the non-stop events that had peppered our lives throughout the fall and into the new year, I thought, *Well no wonder the Lord had quietly slipped a word of warning into my spirit right before it all began.* He had clearly—though not audibly—admonished me saying, "Guard your heart and move forward."

A little puzzled by it, I'd even told Myron and a few others. When those first assaults came my way, I remembered God's warning and thought he was encouraging me to "keep on keepin' on," as the saying goes.

Have you ever had those times where God gives you a great amount of revelation in a matter of seconds? Somehow, he transfers an entire conversation in the blink of an eye. This was one of those times for me.

It happened so rapidly: I remembered saying, "God, I trust you," that night when I had cancer and God gave me breakthrough. I remembered saying, "God, I trust you," the night of the accident and God gave me peace. I remembered hearing that sinister voice say, "She doesn't really trust you."

That dream connected the dots for me. The very thing that Satan attacked was the very thing that I settled in my heart and had even declared to others.

As if Satan said, "Oh really? I'll bide my time while I start slowly planting little seeds of doubt. We'll see if you really trust him."

I see that now, but I didn't see that at the time.

I told Myron one of the reasons why I struggled so much when we moved away from Caleb was because I needed to put Caleb in God's hands and say, "I trust you. I'm taking my hands off and putting him in your hands. You kept him for a reason. I know you're going to continue to take care of him and help him. You told me all those years ago he was your son and I choose to still trust you. You love him even more than I do and will continue to take care of him. Even if I'm not around. He's your son and you love him."

A few days after the emergency surgery, my daily devotional was on Adam and Eve's banishment from the garden of Eden. It was a fresh perspective on an old familiar story. It pointed out that God banishing the couple from the garden was an act of tremendous grace and mercy. Oftentimes we assume it was because he was disgusted with them or something like that. I think that we too quickly forget that it wasn't just rebellion, it was a violation of God's love and the relationship he desired with them.

The true reason for their banishment was quite the opposite of our traditional thinking because it was based on a love we can't comprehend.

If they had been allowed to stay, at some point they would have eaten from the tree of life in the center of the garden. That means for all of eternity, they would have to live in that sinful state with no hope of forgiveness or change possible. They would have to bear the consequences of their decisions *forever*. Instead, God orchestrated events to set in motion the plan for our salvation. In essence he said, "I will come for you. I will win back what was lost and redeem you."

As I pondered that kind of amazing love, my mind went back to those panic-filled hours in the emergency room when I had not handled things very well. How distant, dark, and deep the void seemed at the time. As I looked at it through the lens of Scripture, I realized that God had been a gentleman and let me make a choice once again. Would I dwell on those negative thoughts? Or would I choose to believe that his heart is *still* good and that his promises are *still* true and trustworthy? Would I choose to return to all the GodPrint moments he'd left on our story?

Thankfully, that time, I chose to make a conscious decision to trust him. It wasn't immediate, but a shifting started to take place then. Breakthrough came soon after.

I have a sign that says, "I Choose Joy." I love that it reminds me that I have a choice. Maybe I'll make a new sign and hang it on my bathroom wall to see every new morning. It will say, "I Choose Trust." Because, right here, right now, Satan is a defeated foe. The heart of the Father is still good. He can still be trusted. His thoughts are still higher than my thoughts and his ways are still higher than my ways. His thoughts toward me are still for my good and he still has plans to give me hope and a future. I still choose to trust him.

~From Jenny's private journal

SEE YOU SOON

"**WHEN FACED WITH THE DEATH** of a loved one, we have to face reality. Life is short. But we also have to come face to face with the reality of eternity. We don't like that question because then we're faced with, *Where do we go when this life is over?*

"Life is short and can end unexpectedly. Here one day, gone the next. There's no guarantee on life. We do not know that we will wake up tomorrow morning."

The pastor's words at the funeral for my friend's mom who had just recently died of cancer resonated within my heart. I thought about how Saturday, August 29th, 2015 began like any other morning. None of us could have possibly imagined that Jacob would not live to see another day.

The message made me think of a concept I'd recently heard while listening to an audio version of "Suffer Strong" by Katherine and Jay Wolf. The husband and wife speak from experience, as they've been through some extremely difficult physical challenges when Katherine had a debilitating stroke in her twenties with a newborn baby at home.

They pointed out that we're just as prone to trade the truth of God for a lie as God's people were in ages past, but he's still patiently waiting for us to *remember*. They said that God's trying to tell us, *Remember me! You already know the end of the story—remember me!*

What really struck me, though, was when they named the top five regrets people experience on their death bed:

1. I wish I hadn't worked so hard.
2. I wish I had stayed in touch with my friends.
3. I wish I had let myself be happier.
4. I wish I'd had the courage to express my true self.
5. I wish I'd led a life true to my dreams instead of what others expected of me.

Katherine and Jay's testimony show that suffering and hope, intertwined, can change your life and your perspective going forward.

While I listened to their story, I thought of all the times that I'd heard Pastor Campbell stress the importance of processing life correctly. He'd often said, "If we're going to live this life, we might as well live it well, all the way to the end."

I found myself stopping the audiobook to listen again as they explained a new concept that I hadn't heard of before. I'd heard of PTSD (post-traumatic stress disorder). The grief counselor that I met with right after the accident even thought we might be experiencing it to some degree.

The Wolfs presented a new concept for me to consider. I never knew that there's something called post-traumatic growth.

It also has a "top five" list, but I like this one much better:

1. A renewed appreciation for life
2. New possibilities
3. More personal strength
4. Improved relationships
5. Spiritual satisfaction

They pointed out that trauma can open a different way of living if we process it right. One with fewer regrets at the end of our lives if we choose to allow it to *grow* us. Traumatic events cause all of life's trivial, meaningless things to fall away so we are left with what's truly important.

I thought about my own life and the second chance I had been given. All those times the doctors were concerned that the cancer might have come back. All those times when there was fear that a different kind of cancer would be faced now. Yet there I sat, alive and healthy. Why me? Why do some lose the battle to cancer and some win?

That time of cancer forged something in my life that probably never would have happened any other way. There were even things put into me in my childhood that never would have happened if I had not experienced adversity and struggles.

I can see now how all those things have helped shape me into the person that I am now. Now, when I walk in a room and see someone sitting by themselves looking lonely, I make it a point to go over and introduce myself because I know what that feels like. Now, if I hear of a friend's illness, I reach out to offer encouragement as one who's walked that road. Now, when I learn of a tragic loss, I pray for those left behind as someone who understands the whirlwind of grief coming their way.

If I allow them, those past experiences can be reference points to help me in life. When I chose to give my life to Christ in my teenage years, he began using those experiences to shape me. He's brought deep healing into some of those wounded areas so that I can reach out and help others. Those things that hell would have meant for evil in my childhood, in the hands of Jesus, are turned around. He's able to use them for my good, but also to benefit those around me.

But sometimes it's external forces, even hell, that assault our destiny. In my life, coming from an alcoholic family, battling cancer, and losing a son were deviations from the straight, linear path I had planned for my life. Yet even in all those things, when I invited Jesus in, he was able to teach me things from those experiences and help me to mature.

These detours not only help me become more like Jesus, they give me a chance to judge my own sin before he must. Over and over, Scripture warns us that judgment begins in God's house and with God's people. So, when I consider God's correction now in light of the coming judgment, his grace really does amaze me—that he would patiently work with me *now* to get things right *today* so that one day in the future, I can stand before him clean and unashamed.

As the days turned into weeks, weeks rolled into months, we continue striving to "keep on keepin' on."

It's been years since our world was rocked to the very core. Years since our life was upended and everything that we thought we knew was tested. Years since all our dreams for Jacob were snatched away in a moment of time.

Sometimes I allow myself to go through some of Jacob's things that we kept. As the tears flow, I remember all the holidays we celebrated together—birthday celebrations, family trips. My mother-in-law was right when she told me, "Jenny, those memories hurt now, but one day, they will be precious."

So, when fear tries to overwhelm me, or worry, financial difficulties, health scares, anger, rejection, addiction, whatever may come my way, I must step out in faith and draw closer to Jesus.

Today I refuse to wallow in despair. I refuse to go down in defeat but instead remember all the scriptures which remind us that we are not of those who shrink back from the battle but take it to the very gates of hell.

Today I will remember all his promises for those who endure: he will restore and redeem all things.

All things.

I think of Jacob's poem "Holding Me," and as I look back over my life, I can see the evidence of all the times that God was *holding me*. Even when I couldn't see him. Even when I couldn't feel him. His hand was still holding me, leaving upon my story his God-Prints—heavenly evidence of his never-ending, unfailing love.

As I said at the close of the eulogy for my mom, "Just as our good, heavenly Father was faithful to plan and prepare for Jacob to meet him, I have full confidence that he did the same for my mom. So, Mom, we love you. We miss you terribly. But this isn't farewell forever. This is, 'See you soon.'"

EPILOGUE

THE VIEW WAS SO STUNNING that I had to stop and stare at the wonder—the awe—of it all. I'd just come through the most glorious field I've ever experienced. Bold, vibrant flowers interspersed with tall, elegant amber stocks gently swaying back and forth in the breeze. Beauty doesn't even begin to capture the essence. Once, on a road trip through Kansas, I'd seen "amber waves of grain" swaying in the wind.

I became aware of a delightful fragrance that floated to my senses and reminded me of the beautiful wildflowers I'd seen when I first arrived. Crisp, with a hint of something like citrus? There was something else too—soothing lavender? Or maybe lilacs? For someone like me who loves flowers, the scent was, well . . . heavenly.

But this. Oh, this was beyond anything my mind could ever conceive—the splendor and majesty of it all.

But that wasn't even the best part. No—the best part was that awaiting me on the other side of the meadow—a welcoming party like no other.

People from all walks of life and every color of the rainbow were there to welcome *me*. Some I recognized immediately—my beloved son Jacob and my redeemer Jesus.

Others, though, I had to strain to remember . . . could that be the man that I shared a brief word with? I remember telling him that, "It's not about church. It's not about religion. It's about Jesus. He loves you and wants to heal those hurting, broken places inside you. You can talk to him anywhere, you know? When you're quiet on your bed at night or when you're feeling all alone. He loves you and he cares. Just think about it." I guess he did think about it because he's here too.

Somehow, I knew that there would be plenty of time for me to learn each of their stories and why they were here to greet me.

That simple reunion was already a balm for my weary soul. But this. Oh, this.

As I crested the little rise, I stopped right there as the view took my breath away.

Home.

I'm finally home.

The very place my soul has been craving all along.

No words can adequately describe what I witnessed as I stood there attempting to drink it all in.

Up ahead was an archway—glowing and glistening in iridescent light. Flanking each side were stone walls stretching as far as the eye can see in either direction. The whole thing seemed almost alive as if it glowed with a pulse all its own.

As I came closer, and the view inside the gate came into focus, I became aware of the sounds and scents that were luring me onward too. Laughter—raucous, belly-hurting laughter—floated over the walls to my ears. Music and singing.

Joy. It's like the sound of joy swept into my being and became a force of its own.

And the smells. Oh, they tantalized my senses, bringing my

appetite roaring to life. Some delicious roasting aroma wafted over to me and caused me to pause right there and breathe in deeply, capturing the scent of pure, delighted satisfaction.

Slowly, I became aware of other wonderful scents too. I've never savored frankincense before, but somehow, I knew that's what the fragrance was. Not a suffocating, overwhelming odor—but soothing. Inviting me to sit a spell and linger in its restorative powers.

I realized I had completely stopped, right there outside the beautiful gate.

Who was waiting for me inside? What was waiting for me on the other side of that threshold?

As I stood there, still dumbfounded to finally be *home*, Jacob appeared. It startled me at first because he had not been there a moment ago. I quickly adjusted though as a calm reassurance rested my heart and reminded me that this is the way of my new home.

Home. My new *home.*

As Jacob reached for my hand and began tugging me forward, practically skipping down the street through that awe-inspiring gate, I almost stumbled as I caught my first glimpse of what was beyond the archway. So much had been hidden beyond those walls. Walls that I thought resplendent paled in comparison to the absolute wonder in front of me.

As far across the horizon as I could see, the city stretched. All at once, it looked like pictures I'd seen of ancient cities with cobblestone streets. Wait. Did the street just shine? No, it's more like the stones winked at me in their brilliance. The walls of the houses and shops looked like ancient Middle Eastern dwellings with their carved-from-nature appearance. Yet, on second glance, so much more inviting and welcoming. Even more—the color! Such a burst of color—everywhere: Flowers, banners, signs, curtains flapping in the gentle breeze blowing through open windows. Cheerful voices of shared conversations floated through open doorways.

People of all shapes, sizes, and complexion strolled down the streets, pausing occasionally as if on a leisurely vacation, to peruse merchandise or be regaled with a shopkeeper's tale.

Occasionally an animal darted, unnoticed, down a side street or two. Dogs, cats, was that a lion that just bounded across the road? My heart leaped inside of me until I noticed that no one seemed to care. No one even seemed to take note. The lion continued and then disappeared around a corner. All this time, life moved forward, which was odd to me. I began to shrug in amazement as a hand clasped mine once again.

"Mom."

Almost in impatience, but in more of a humoring tone, as if to say, "I know—pretty incredible, isn't it?"

"Mom, come here. I want to show you something."

I blinked to clear my thoughts and refocus. For a moment there, I'd been completely absorbed in drinking in the astonishing sights around me that I had not even heard Jacob speaking to me. Jacob? Oh, yes! Jacob!

"What was that, son?"

"Look!" he cried out, as he turned me around—pivoting me away from the view that captivated me.

"Are those mountains in the city?"

"What? Oh, yeah! Mom, the city is huge. It goes on for days and days. I'm not sure how far away those mountains are. I haven't been there . . . yet."

While he turned me around, I glanced once more at the distant peaks, twinkling in dotted snow. They seemed to reflect radiance from . . . where? Not the mountain's top, as they would if they were reflecting the sun. *Hm.* It's like they glowed from light all around them.

"C'mon, Mom." Jacob chuckled as he finally succeeded in getting me completely turned around. I wanted to stay right there, in the middle of the street, soaking it all in. Why was he turning me around? What could possibly be so striking behind me that could rival such beauty before me?

As I turned, my jaw dropped in astonishment. On the backside of those magnificent walls—who looks at the *backside* of a wall?—was art beyond compare. To call it a mural is a grave injustice. Turning to the left and right, I could see artisans positioned with their materials every so often all along my field of vision. Each one was diligently at work on their portion of this masterpiece. No craftsman's supplies were the same as another's: some chiseled, some painted, some engraved, some sketched. Some were even weaving fabric or cloth of some sort *into* the wall itself. You would think it would be gaudy, but the overall effect was stunning.

Beautiful humming resonated through the atmosphere as each slowly and meticulously crafted a portion of the wall into a unique work of art. Somehow, though, each individual design was intricately woven into the designs around it in a seamless fashion.

Yet again, I was snapped out of my dazed stupor as Jacob grinned and pulled me forward.

"Wait until I show you what Grandad and I have been working on. The King says it will all be finished by the time the Wedding Supper of the Lamb begins."

As he dragged me onward, almost dancing in excitement, I shook my head and chuckled to *myself* this time.

Wedding Supper of the Lamb? These are things I've read about, heard about, even taught Sunday school children about. But I'm *here*. And it's *really* happening.

"The King says that it's almost time too. All who have been invited are on their way. Just as soon as the last one who accepted the invitation arrives, the celebration begins."

My feet left the pavement for the luscious, grassy hillside embankment that led to a distant spot along the wall. Jacob continued to tug me onward with, "C'mon."

The soft grass seemed almost alive and life-giving itself. I glanced around, not wanting to miss a chance to drink in a different view of this incredible place. Indescribable. Like the plains of

Africa on a safari that I'd been on before. But . . . there. That latest view of the landscape brought to mind the charming country park near where we lived once.

Little lakes dotted the area where even more people were . . . fishing? Yes.

And the trees. Oh, the trees were glorious in their own right. Each tall, majestic one was different, yet marvelous to behold. I stood still for a moment contemplating exactly what kind of fruit hung on the low branches near me.

Suddenly, I was being pulled forward again with another, "C'mon. It's just over this little rise, Mom. We're almost there."

At that moment, it's like all else faded away and a thought thunderbolted through my mind—sharp and precise in its clarity.

Another walk in another park, many years before.

It almost seemed like a distant, elusive memory that I couldn't quite make out completely. More like a grainy flashback, yet it remained.

Wandering through a park before, getting lost in thoughts tumbling through my mind.

That park was a place of death though. A final resting place for the shells of precious souls who completed their earthly journey.

But *this*? This place was life. *Life* everywhere.

Then I just *knew*. I knew that I could spend all of eternity exploring this place and never grow bored. I could spend millennia talking with Moses, Rahab, Mary Magdalene, and Simon Peter and never scratch the surface of all the insight I could glean.

Even more so, though, I knew that my deepest longing, the desire of my heart, had been met in this place.

I am known and I am accepted.

I am loved and I belong here.

My beautiful Savior has made a way for me to be here—*forever*.

I can't wait to see what else awaits me just over the rise.

LETTER TO THE READER

I LOVE STORIES WHERE THE underdog, the least likely to overcome, succeeds. Surmounting obstacles, resisting defeat, right up to the bloody finish line. Refusing to admit defeat. Maybe because I secretly hope that "Yes, if they could overcome that, I can overcome this."

Maybe that's why I'm continually drawn to stories of triumph over great adversity. Or stories of great heroism and courage even in the face of death.

When I share our story, I'm always amazed at how people are amazed. I mean, I know little old me. Nothing special here. Just Jenny trying to live for Jesus, make heaven my home, and help as many others find their way home too.

But maybe they're really drawn to the hope that perhaps they can overcome too. I mean hey, if the Leavitt family can go through all of that, there's hope for all of us, right?

In this bird's-eye view of our family's story, I chose to add some scenes from heaven's vantage point to remind us of the very real battle we've been born into. An epic battle with a Conquering King and brand-new kingdom coming soon.

Our question to you—are you ready for the kingdom of Heaven? Are you ready to stand before the King?

You can be.

The King who went to hell and back said to choose wisely.

The stakes are high.

Eternity weighs in the balance.

Build your life on the solid Rock while there's still time.

Just talk to Jesus and say something like this:

> *Lord Jesus,* I come before you. I know that it wasn't the nails that kept you on the cross. It was your love for sinners like me. You took my place and the punishment I deserve. Please forgive me of my sin—the wrongs I've committed that have put distance between us.
>
> I surrender. I am done trying this on my own. I want to walk uprightly before you. I don't care what people think; I don't care what people say. I don't care what other people do. God, I just want you.
>
> God, I want all of you, so I'm giving you all of me.
>
> I don't care about the worldly things. God, I want to be in Your will, and I ask you to forgive me from holding back from you. God, I want everything you have for me, and so I'm surrendering my life to you. Have it. Take it. Use it. Spend me for Your glory. I'm so grateful that you knew me before the universe was ever created and adopted me into Your family.
>
> In Jesus's name,
>
> Amen!

If you've settled it with Christ, like I did so many years ago, then I can't wait to meet you in the new kingdom. What a day that will be!

Finally, dear friends, thank you. We recognize that there are many things you could have done with your time, but you chose to spend it following along with us as we shared our story. What a gift!

From our family to yours,

The Leavitts

*When we enter into a personal relationship with
Jesus, our name is added to Heaven.
God will refresh and give courage to the repentant
and humble heart.*
—Jacob Leavitt's personal notes from Pastor Jeremy Meyer's
sermon "What do you want?" (4/17/2013)

ACKNOWLEDGMENTS

THANK YOU TO EVERYONE WHO has walked alongside our family through the valley of the shadow of death. We could not have done this alone. Your prayers, love, and concern for us gave us strength to keep moving forward.

I thank God for our beloved church family, Victory Chapel, in Jacksonville, Florida. They've shown the world what "love for the brethren" really means as they shared all of life with us: the good, the bad, and everything in between.

We are so blessed to have such Spirit-filled, God-fearing leadership who has walked each step of this journey with us. You've wept right alongside us in the throes of our intense grief. And you've rejoiced with us as we've seen our God turn all things for our good and his glory.

I am extremely grateful for our Senior Pastor, Ron Meyer. His wholehearted obedience and devotion to God shines in his faithfulness to God and God's people. Pastor, from the day you met Myron on the navy base in 1992, you and your family have been an integral part of our lives. Your words of wisdom are woven throughout the pages of this book just as your love for God overflowed from your hearts to ours. "Thank you" just doesn't seem adequate for how grateful we are that you answered the call, packed up your family, and moved 3,000 miles across the country into the unknown to answer God's call. You challenge us to a high level of love and service to our wonderful and personal Savior; yet you also come alongside us in our times of failure (there have been many!) and continually reach out with a heart to see our lives restored.

I thank God for our pastor's wife, Bridget, as well. Not only has she taught me to listen to, and do my best to obey, God's voice; she has also been an example of a woman striving to be what God called her to be. Day in and day out, Bridget, you've been faithful to him and a shining example of a woman who loves Jesus and supports her husband's calling. On top of that, your friendship means more to me than I can ever say. I'm so grateful for you, Bridget!

Our Assistant Pastor Jeremy Meyer: Just as your dad (Pastor Ron Meyer) has been an integral part of our lives over the last thirty years, you've been right there too. From the moment you and Myron knocked on my family's front door to invite me out to that little concert in the park, your testimony, leadership, and friendship have proven to be a treasure to us. Only eternity will tell the power of a life laid down in service to the King.

Tiffany Meyer: Ever since the day we met, I've appreciated your steadfast heart for God and your willingness to lay down your dreams and desires to see what God will do with your yielded heart. I feel so privileged to have witnessed you grow into the strong woman of God that you are today. You are a true friend who has—literally—been there in my darkest hour. You have my deep and abiding gratitude for your friendship.

Our beloved leadership Pastor Joe Campbell and his wife, Connie: You both have been a shining example of a marriage who not only survived the loss of a child but chose to let that loss draw you closer to each other and Jesus. The healing then flowed through you to others–including us. Thank you! We needed to see that a marriage can not only survive, but even thrive, after such devastating loss. Thank you also for pouring into Pastor Ron and Bridget

Meyer, who in turn, poured into us. We hope and pray to continue the pattern and pour out our own lives into those God brings our way.

I am eternally grateful for the new friends God has brought our way since our lives changed to "before and after." Albert and Yolie Martinez, along with their daughter, Veronica Diaz, have been a godsend to us, and we are forever grateful for their love, support, kindness, and listening ear. Their friendship is priceless to us.

To my faithful friend Amy Bonser: You have been such an encouragement to me through this whole process that thank you seems inadequate. Every word you said—whether to inspire me, to challenge me to think from a different angle, whatever the case may be—was because you believed in me and believed in this book. May God return the love right back at you, my friend!

I would like to thank these dedicated Christian professionals for loving Jesus first (and others a close second). Our lives are better, in part, because of you allowing Christ's comfort and healing to flow through you into our lives. Thank you for being vessels he was able to use during a difficult season in our lives—Dr. Dennis Blanchette, Jennifer Weldon, and Alisa Grove.

There are so many more that have continually shown love and care for us through the years that we could write another book and still not thank them all! I pray that the Lord repay you in multiplied blessings, both in this life and in the Heaven to come.

Words cannot express how grateful I am for my husband, Myron. I'm so proud to be your wife! Thank you for being my partner, friend, and lover on this journey! Always an adventure, babe!

To Caleb: What can I say, son? I am so proud to be your mom! Like I said in the pages of this book—you are a young man after God's heart who is striving to love him, serve him, and make a difference in this generation! Keep on fightin,' mighty warrior for God—till the end!

To Jacob: I pray that our Lord allows you to see the fruit that will come as we share our family's story. We are committed to not giving up on this generation, son. May God use your words and testimony to touch people's lives even beyond the grave. We eagerly await our reunion one day soon! Hope you're ready to be our tour guide!

And to Jesus: "Thank you" seems so inadequate . . . How can I express how grateful I am to you? You graciously give me your love and forgiveness and ask for nothing in return but my surrendered heart. I give it to you freely. May this book be an offering to you and may you be able to use our testimony for your glory and your Name's sake. I love you, Jesus.

CREDITS

I'M ONE OF THOSE RARE and nerdy people who actually read the acknowledgments and credits in the back of a book. I've always wondered why authors gush over their editors so much in those pages. Now I understand! Putting together a project like this is a monumental task that I could not have done alone. I'm indebted to the team that helped me with everything from mentoring, to editing, to putting it all together and publishing.

Alycia Morales—my mentor who pushed me to mine the deep hurts for God's handiwork and the lessons that he taught me through those trials. Those lessons became reference points to help prepare me—us—for the greatest trial to come.

The talented editing team at Called Writers: Chris and Shannon McKinney and Holly Crawshaw were an absolute godsend to me. They helped me weed through the "fluff" and hone the story to what you see today. Any wordy, redundant sections are entirely on me! Holly: I cannot recommend you more highly—you and I both know exactly what a hot mess this manuscript was before you agreed to tackle it. I am not exaggerating when I say that it would not be what it is today without you applying your God-given gifts to it (2 Corinthians 2:8–14, my friend),

The Word Weavers (Volusia) group not only took me in as one

of their own but supported and encouraged me every step of the way.

Lastly, it is not possible to count how many podcasts I listened to trying to learn this whole "writing thing." The two that were vital in this process were both hosted by Thomas Umstadtt Jr. and were absolutely free. *The Christian Publishing Show* and the *Novel Marketing Podcast* provided me with tangible resources to navigate my way through this huge learning curve.

May God bless each one of these precious people for their heart to teach, train, and guide others. Without each of them, I have serious doubts that this book would have ever been finished.

Thank you!

About the Leavitts

Myron Leavitt is the pastor of Victory Chapel in Sanford, Florida, just north of Orlando. He also works in management for a security-monitoring corporation. He's learned much in life through the School of Hard Knocks; yet those same difficult life lessons are what God has used to shape him into the man and leader that he is. The trials he's experienced in this life have brought a depth of character and compassion for others that wouldn't have come any other way. He continues to preach the Good News wherever the Lord leads.

Jenny Leavitt is a pastor's wife who has written for ministry publications for years but never considered that "real" writing. She just did it because she loved it and there was a need. Now, she serves alongside her husband in a community desperate for Good News, where she continues to be amazed at how far God will go to rescue broken, hurting people. She wrote this book after feeling compelled to share her family's story of God's faithfulness through shattering loss. She continues to encourage others to lean into Jesus in all of life's ups and downs and in-betweens.

Caleb Leavitt is currently an elementary school teacher in Orange Park, Florida. He's learned that every day with God is a day of new beginnings. He endeavors to make the most of this second chance at life that God gave him as he trusts him to work "all things for good" for those that love him. He boldly shares his story of healing and redemption to anyone who cares to hear.

All three of the Leavitts are passionate about Jesus and believe in sharing his love with everyone God brings into their sphere of influence. They will continue to "labor while it is yet day" to bring as many precious souls to heaven with them as they can.

The family is eternally grateful for the coming reunion with Jacob—and all of their other loved ones who have gone before them to glory. What an exciting day that will be!

Want to Know More?

Find exclusive content, bonus features, resource recommendations, the family's photo gallery, and more at jennyleavitt.com.

Do you know a father, son, or brother who could use a man's perspective on grief, loss, survivor's guilt, and overcoming life's broken areas? Connect with Myron and Caleb at jennyleavitt.com as well.

The Leavitts' heart is to come alongside the hurting who don't think there will ever be hope again and journey with you as you discover what we already have: hope is available. Let us help you find it.

Connect with us at jennyleavitt.com.

We'd love to get to know you!

1 Thessalonians 4:15–18

For this we declare to you by a word from the Lord, that we who are alive, who are left until the coming of the Lord, will not precede those who have fallen asleep. For the Lord himself will descend from heaven with a cry of command, with the voice of an archangel, and with the sound of the trumpet of God. And the dead in Christ will rise first. Then we who are alive, who are left, will be caught up together with them in the clouds to meet the Lord in the air, and so we will always be with the Lord. Therefore encourage one another with these words.

You Can Help!

Want to help share the same hope and encouragement you received?

Here are two simple things you can do to help spread the story of *GodPrints*:

1. If you enjoyed this book, write a positive review and post it at online retailers and websites.
2. Recommend this book to a friend, a book club, your local library—anywhere you think it will impact lives.

We value your opinion! If you post a review, please share it with us at jennyleavitt.com.